Structural Ambiguity
in Brahms

Analytical Approaches
to Four Works

Studies in British Musicology

Nigel Fortune, Series Editor
Professor of Music
The University of Birmingham

Structural Ambiguity in Brahms

Analytical Approaches to Four Works

by
Jonathan Dunsby

RESEARCH PRESS

Produced and distributed by
UMI Research Press
an imprint of
University Microfilms International
Ann Arbor, Michigan 48106

A revision of the author's thesis,
Leeds University, 1976

Library of Congress Cataloging in Publication Data

Dunsby, Jonathan.
    Structural ambiguity in Brahms.

    (British studies in Musicology)
    "A revision of the author's thesis, Leeds University,
1976."
    Bibliography: p.
    Includes index.
    1. Brahms, Johannes, 1833-1897. Works.   I. Title.
II. Series.

MT92.B81D86 1981   780'.92'4   81-24
ISBN 0-8357-1159-5

Contents

Preface

Much of this study's analysis is in the form of diagrams and musical examples that give both quotation and analytical sketches. Diagrams, using conventional shorthand for harmony (e.g., I–V), tonality (e.g., c:), proportion (e.g., 8 + 8) and so on, are unnumbered: they are relevant in the sequence of the text, and are not referred to elsewhere. Musical examples are figured consecutively throughout each chapter: references (e.g., 'see Figure 1') are therefore relevant only to the sequence within a chapter. Although the notation in musical examples varies according to analytical demands, certain usages are consistent. Staves with no initial brace are always analytical: no direct quotation from the score is without a brace and an initial bar number. Bar numbers in examples are given in brackets: numbers not appearing in brackets are analytical, often referring to degrees of scalic progression. In both diagrams in the text and musical examples, harmonic relationships, denoted by Roman numerals, are not distinguished by mode: thus 'I', for example, denotes either tonic major or tonic minor. Where modality is relevant to the analysis, a verbal explanation is given.

In the text, bar numbers are referred to without prefix (e.g., 'in 1–23'). Specific beats are indicated by a figure above and following the bar number (e.g., 1^2–3^4).

The occasional foreign references appear in the original language. The extracts from Brahms's letters in Appendix I, however, are also given in translation.

Few of the ideas motivating this study could have been developed without the help of Professor Alexander Goehr. His generous sharing of a profound understanding of music is gratefully acknowledged. No tribute could convey the debt owed to Anne for her countless forms of help over the years when this book was conceived, written, and published.

1

Introduction

Although a detailed argument is not pursued through the following chapters, the sequence of analyses and discussions falls into a natural progression. The concern running through all the studies is musical ambiguity. Brahms's music is characterized by an avoidance of straightforward relationships. There may often be a simple aesthetic framework for his ideas, for example, in periodic phrasing (discussed in Chapter 5). At some level of the structure, however, Brahms usually creates a functional ambiguity, giving his music its typically elaborate and complex character.

It seems appropriate to begin with an examination of ambiguous relationships, in a context which minimizes other considerations. Cases of simple, ambiguous formation are created by isolating the first two bars of each variation in the *Handel Variations*. These are analyzed as a complex of binary oppositions. A graphic model is formulated for each type of ambiguous structure, and the results are tabulated to see whether there is any pattern through the work.

This approach was stimulated by Brahms's recorded views on variation technique, which are far from self-explanatory. Geiringer, for example, is led to make a claim which is hard to identify in Brahms's music:

> ...Brahms's demand that the bass must be the bearer of the harmony, or, put more simply, that the harmony of the Theme must be clearly recognizable in the Variations...[1]

The analysis in Chapter 2 may go some way to clarifying Brahms's intention and practice.

The following chapter focuses on harmonic and tonal ambiguity in a more conventional approach. Although the Piano Quartet movement which is examined is not central to the Brahms repertoire, it is an intriguing case of the concurrence of two unorthodox formal features. The unconventional tonality of the recapitulation is presumed to have a necessary function in the movement, and it is suggested that this relies on fundamental ambiguities in the tonal procedure. The description of a tonal scheme characterized by long passages of static tonality explains why the equally unorthodox idea of tonally static variation in the second subject is appropriate.

The third analytical account again changes the focus by examining a conflict in the formal procedure of the first movement from the *Fourth Symphony*. The movement is not easily analyzed in terms of sonata convention, though several writers, for example Harrison, do so:

> (Unlike the Passacaglia-Finale)...the first three movements of the Fourth all adhere(d) to that symphonic enlargement of what is termed sonata form; that is, each movement has its exposition, development, recapitulation and final coda.[2]

This only reveals the obvious contrasts of the work. Prompted, perhaps, by an observation that the Finale has in any case the background of an exposition, development, recapitulation and coda, Evans made the more penetrating observation[3] that there are similar procedures in the first and last movements. This is also discussed by Rostand, who notes that the principal theme recurs in transformed versions, in the 'spirit of the chaconne'.[4] Neither writer gives a full account of how it is that Chaconne and sonata procedure are combined. The present analysis attempts to show that a tension between these procedures generates the proportions of the movement and many detailed ambiguities.

Finally, Schoenberg's view of Brahms's development of the musical language is examined, with supplementary examples. Two concerns prompted this closing chapter. First, in view of the shortage of relatively modern analytical discussion of Brahms, it would be unfortunate in principle to ignore the views, recorded in *Brahms the Progressive,* of a composer and theorist of Schoenberg's stature. Both Brahms and Schoenberg were acutely aware of their relationship to the Viennese tradition: Schoenberg's insight into Brahms was motivated by an obvious sympathy. Second, Schoenberg's essay, in its elaborate account of the developing musical language from Mozart to his own time, touches on many issues which are raised in the earlier chapters. Assessments of historical position have been avoided as far as possible in the analyses. It is hoped, therefore, that the confrontation of analysis and Schoenberg's assessment of Brahms will show the two approaches to be mutually supportive.

2

Variations on a Theme by Handel, Op. 24

INTRODUCTION

Brahms did not often record his views about composition, yet on two occasions, some 13 years apart, he wrote emphatically about the need for some kind of strict technique in Variations.[1] It seems that conventional analytical approaches would not be able to break Brahms's code, for he writes in the conventional language of the time. Taking 'bass' in its normal meaning, his comments are inconsistent, and in any case hardly representative of his music.

The common type of motivic analysis seems particularly limited in this context: an emphasis on the melodic elements is just what Brahms himself tried to avoid. Similarly, Variations are not amenable to the kind of harmonic approach which is useful in dealing with tonal forms (like sonata form). More sophisticated methods are needed, and perhaps the most sophisticated and relatively modern source would be Schenker, who applied his theories[2] to a wide range of forms and styles. But Schenker does not deal as convincingly with Variations as with tonal forms, because his analysis is based on the characteristics of prolonged tonal relationships: Variations do not normally have a significant tonal structure. Schenker does not mention the *Ursatz* or "fundamental structure" in his brief reference to Variations in *Free Composition,*[3] and is not, therefore, wholly explaining the form. And Jonas, a Schenkerian apologist, relies on dogma: 'Die Idee der Variationskunst ist ohne die Idee eines Ursatzes...gar nicht denkbar.'[4]

In his analysis of Reger's *Variations and Fugue on a Theme by J.S. Bach, Op. 81*[5] Schenker considers only the nature of each variation and its relationship to the Theme. He seems to ignore the overall structure of the piece, which in other contexts is his highest priority.

The question — what is the continuing element in Variations? — has rarely been investigated. Nelson attempted to define general laws for variation technique, and he discovered in the post-Baroque variation a:

> ...principle, valid for (the) structural techniques...The melodic subject and the harmonico-structural frame are complementary phenomena: alterations of the melodic subject are balanced by a relatively close adherence to the harmonico-structural frame; conversely, the literal retention of the melodic subject is offset by harmonic departures within the harmonico-structural frame, as well as by figural or contrapuntal involvement of the supporting voices.[6]

It is revealing that Nelson is happy to specify 'alteration of the melodic subject', but avoids such a positive function as 'alteration of the harmonico-structural frame'. The difficulty lies in defining the frame and its function — where is it in the music? is it used as a model for composition? or is it perceived as a repeated background for each variation?

This lack of consistency is not uncommon in analytical studies. It often arises through the attempt to translate music into verbal concepts. It may be interesting instead to build an analogue, or a model, of the music. This would present the musical structure in an abstract and consistent metaphor. Above all, it should be competent to reconcile different kinds of analysis (e.g. harmonic analysis with what might be called 'comparative' melodic analysis which shows motivic similarities). Only such a consistency enables the analysis to show which elements of the musical structure are formative. The alternative is the usual controversy, with one side claiming that motivic relationships are most formative, and the other appealing to form, harmony and so on. Meyer makes the point strongly, if not clearly:

> ...analytical methods such as those developed by Schenker, Lorenz and Kurth, as well as more traditional ones, all essentially aim at exhibiting the hierarchic-functional structure of musical events. While emphasizing the importance of hierarchic structure, the systematic formulations and practical procedures of analytic theory have tended to neglect and underestimate the significance of differences among hierarchic levels within particular works. That is, theorists have...often assumed that the principles of hierarchic organization remain constant from level to level. But...the particular parameters of sound used to articulate process and structure will vary in kind as well as in emphasis from one level to another.[7]

In order to create such a model, the articulation of each structural level will be examined. It will show only the articulatory hierarchy, and so be an abstract model of the music. It may be regarded as what linguistics terms a 'synthetic' model, which cannot be used to generate 'well-formed' messages without the addition of an available language (often called 'content' in music).

Articulation will be regarded as a function of repetition, an idea inspired by Ruwet.[8] He puts the problem of actually defining repetition in a sensible perspective, by acknowledging and discounting the logic that:

> ...du point de vue purement physique, deux événements concrets ne sont jamais complètement identiques.[9]

Ruwet divides musical elements, to be considered in terms of repetition, into 'parametrical' and 'non-parametrical' qualities. The characteristic of parametrical elements is that they define contrasting, successive divisions of the music (either repetitive or non-repetitive) by simple binary oppositions.[10] Non-parametrical elements show a great number of distinctions (on any one level).[11]

Ruwet considers only non-parametrical elements. In Brahms this is almost unavoidable, as parametrical oppositions are rarely of great importance on a detailed level. In a few cases in our analysis, however, parametrical oppositions are included because they show a significant distinction between Theme and Variation.

The fundamental difference between the present method and that of Ruwet is that he divides his material strictly according to its repetitions, whereas here the material is already considered to be divided by its conventional (i.e., harmonic, melodic) articulation: these conventional divisions are classed simply according to their oppositional status. It is possible here to use repetition as a strict articulatory determinant; but it may also be misdirected, for we assume that conventionally structured information is more significant than phenomenal information. The definition of structure in this context is not systematic, but it has a guiding principle — the distinction between 'event' and 'idea'. A musical event becomes an idea when it emerges from its meaningless background, that is, when it sets up a meaningful expectation. For example, Eflat–D, the first two notes of the first melody in Mozart's *Symphony in G minor, K550,* is not an idea; it is part of a 'background' series of notes, the chromatic scale, which can be continued at will; in setting up this expectation it contracts, according to our *ad hoc* definition, no musical meaning. The notes Eflat–D–D, however, do form an idea, for the automatic motion of the background is interrupted. The articulation of ideas in this sense will be the object of analysis. In other words the comparative, co-ordinating method is applied to information which is structured *a priori,* normally in a conventional way. One example of these conventions (from Mozart) is given above: another would be the grouping together of three chords as I–V–I (which, being a structured harmonic idea, might be compared with the subsequent progression to see whether the two are opposed [e.g., I–V–I/IV–II–VI] or non-opposed [I–V–I/I–V–I]).

The Mozart example serves as an introduction to the system of notation. The first two notes would not normally be considered, as they merely form an event. However, being different notes, they are opposed (O): as this is a relationship of pitch, they would appear in the melodic level (m) of the structure as:

mO

Dealing with the first idea (Eflat–D–D), we would look at its relationship to the next one: in this case there is an exact repetition, so the ideas are melodically non-opposed (mnO). They are also non-opposed rhythmically, and these two (simultaneous) functions are co-ordinated vertically in the oppositional diagram:

Figure 1

These simple terms — O, nO, and m, r and h (harmonic level) — are the basic kinds of articulation and structural levels: vertical co-ordination in a diagram signifies simultaneous function.

The first complication comes in dealing with oppositional relationships which are not absolute. There is no literal opposition in music, for events which are perceived independently have at least that quality in common: in one respect at least they are similar rather than opposed. Ruwet avoided too exact a definition of repetition: similarly, the above logic may be suspended in the face of musical ideas which are clearly designed to oppose each other. The hallmark of Brahms, however, is subtle variation: for example, two melodic ideas may be only slightly different in terms of pitch, and rhythmically similar. Thus we would identify a rhythmic non-opposition (rnO) and a reinforcing (i.e., not absolute) melodic non-opposition (+mnO). A relationship which reinforces another must also act to reduce it. But it is normally impossible to claim that there is an equal quantity of two kinds of articulation; either one supplements the other, or they tend to set up a conflicting articulation. Reinforcement may have its literal opposite in reduction, but there can be no such thing as a negative musical effect.

A more basic complication is simply the expression of repetition in terms of opposition, for it uses reversed terms:

repetition = non-opposition

non-repetition = opposition

This switch has been made to accommodate the dimension of time, for opposition can apply to time as well as to musical elements. Thus successive musical elements can be considered to be temporally opposed (tO) and simultaneous ones to be temporally non-opposed (tnO). Often this distinction plays no significant role in the analysis. Normal temporal functions can be expressed in the vertical layout of the diagrammatic model: for instance,

$$
\begin{array}{ll}
\text{i)} & \dfrac{\text{O}}{} \\
\text{ii)} & \text{nO:nO}
\end{array}
$$

would signify an ambiguous structure with conflicting binary (i) and ternary (ii) articulations, the divisions of which can clearly not be simultaneous. With canon, however, the temporal dislocation, of ideas whose relationship depends on the fact that they are successive, must be expressed (by the function tO): similarly, at one stage Brahms separates the two kinds of articulation which have so far provided structural ambiguity — they are no longer simultaneous (tnO) but successive (tO). Time is regarded, therefore, as concrete: if our terminology is taken to be consistent, time is distinguished from itself (tO). Once again, this problematic logic may be suspended if that allows us to build intelligible and comparable models of musical structure.

The material for these analytical methods is not an intact piece of music, but the first two bars of the Theme and selected variations in the *Handel Variations*. The choice was between a detailed picture of this material and a more general analysis of the complete music, and choosing the former introduces a certain abstraction.[12] The concept of opposition is most useful when it applies to the simplest information. The complications of dealing with parametrical relationships impose a sharp limit on its efficiency, a fact implicit in Ruwet's analyses, where he selects just two parameters. But this small-scale objectivity quickly reveals certain characteristic ambiguities in Brahms, as well as his shunning of literal repetition. So if the method gives only a limited picture of the *Handel Variations*, it focuses in detail on typical examples of Brahms's structure.

ANALYSIS

Aria

The first two bars of the *Aria* are articulated by exact rhythmic repetition of bar 1 by bar 2, exact repetition of harmonic pace, similar melodic structures of repeated rhythmic patterns and similar harmonic structures of repeated rhythmic patterns. These relationships define a binary model:

$$\begin{array}{c} rnO \\ +mnO \\ \underline{+hnO} \end{array}$$

The reinforcing functions (melodic and harmonic) also tend to oppose this primary division in the same way on both levels:

1) m ———— Bflat   C   D   D-Eflat/   D   C   D   D-Eflat

$$O_{(i)} \qquad\qquad\qquad\qquad O_{(ii)}$$

(The first division (i) results from an interruption of the upward scale by a re-peating D: the second (ii) also results from an interrupting D, disturbing the pat-tern: D–auxiliary note–D–auxiliary note–D–D̲)

2) h ———— I   V   I   I V   /   I^c V   I   V^7

          unstable   unst.   unst.   unst.

                  stable   stable

              O   O

There are two points of melodic opposition and two of harmonic opposition. It will be noted that the harmonic level has been analyzed in terms of the expectation aroused by chords (unstable–stable = hO) rather than by equating similar chords. These two levels show a ternary articulation:

$$\begin{array}{c} \overline{mO{:}O} \\ hO{:}O \end{array}$$

The two divisions of the model are now superimposed. The division shown by functions above the line is always the primary division, the lower division always secondary:

$$\begin{array}{c} rnO \\ +mnO \\ \underline{+hnO} \\ mO{:}O \\ hO{:}O \end{array}$$

The symbol ':' joins two points of articulation, implying that there is no significant division on that level between those two points.

Variation 1

For this variation the rhythmic level must be split up: 'r' signifies the overall rhythmic structure, as in the *Aria;* 'rl' will refer to the rhythmic structure of the melody. In this variation there are continuous semiquavers, so the 'r' level has no articulation within the model, and is excluded from it. The detailed characteristics of the melodic structure are altered: for instance, the first two crotchets of the melody in the *Aria* were melodically opposed (Bflat–Ctrill), but are now in reinforcing melodic non-opposition (Bfl–A–Bfl/ C–Bfl–C). These changes, however, do not transform the basic melodic articulation, with its binary division across the bar-line. Similarly, the harmonic level has its original form. The model of Variation 1 is therefore:

$$
\begin{array}{l}
\text{rlnO} \\
+\text{mnO} \\
\underline{+\text{hnO}} \\
\text{mO:O} \\
\text{hO:O}
\end{array}
$$

A comparison with the model of the *Aria* shows that this is a simple variation. The 'r' structure has been eliminated (by setting up a continuous semiquaver pattern), and the other functions are preserved. It is noted in passing that this is an example of what Brahms calls melodic variation. He claims that such variation creates nothing really 'new'.[13]

Variation 2

The rhythmic elimination is carried a stage further, for there is no significant oppositional condition of either r or rl. The primary division is ternary:

Figure 2

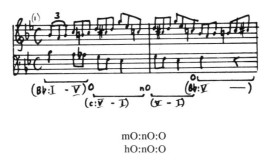

$$
\begin{array}{l}
\text{mO:nO:O} \\
\underline{\text{hO:nO:O}}
\end{array}
$$

But the music is now working against the background of the *Aria* and Variation 1, which were both divided at the bar-line. The model must take account of two secondary structures — the melody and harmony in bar 1 and the melody and harmony in bar 2. At the point of articulation — the bar-line — they seem to be opposed, beginning:

Figure 3

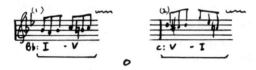

But as the internal repetition gives them similarity, these secondary divisions are classed only as reinforcement (+). The model for Variation 2 is therefore:

$$mO:nO:O$$
$$hO:nO:O$$
$$\overline{}$$
$$+mO$$
$$+hO$$

The primary division of the *Aria* is still strong, as a binary division at the bar-line runs vertically through the diagram. But by using it between structures only half as long as in the original (note that the nO in Figure 2 operates only between beats 3 and 4 of bar 1 and beats 1 and 2 of bar 2), Brahms has allowed his primary division to become ternary. So the binary/ternary hierarchy of the *Aria* and Variation 1 is now inverted to ternary/binary.

The pattern of transformations from the beginning has grown more complex, first with a simple rhythmic elimination, then with a more radical elimination and a basic transformation of the structural hierarchy:

1)   r eliminated

2)   r and r1 eliminated, $\dfrac{O}{O:O}$ replaced by $\dfrac{O:O}{O}$

Variation 4

This is similar to Variation 2. The primary division is ternary, with a binary background:

Figure 4

the model being:

$$mO:nO:O \ ^{14}$$
$$hO:nO:O$$
$$\underline{r2O:nO:O}$$
$$+mO$$
$$+ hO$$
$$+r2O$$

(where 'r2' signifies the rhythmic structure of the bass, which could have been included in Variation 2, but which is especially prominent in this case).

    There is the same non-opposition between the two beats on either side of the bar-line as in Variation 2. However, surrounding this there are two similar relationships:

$$+mnO$$
$$+ hnO$$
$$\underline{+r2nO}$$

which apply to beats 1 and 2 of bar 1 and beats 3 and 4 of bar 2. Thus the primary division has two distinct divisions between three similarly articulated structures (1, 2 and 3 in Figure 4).

    The progress of the primary divisions so far shows a strengthening of the transformations from binary to ternary articulation. By Variation 4 each group of the ternary structure has its own articulation:

Aria	Variation 2	Variation 4
O	O:O	$+nO:nO: + nO$

Variation 6

1)   The h structure is eliminated by a two-part setting.

2)   In contrast to the previous simple articulation, the binary division
     of the model is realized by weak functions in a context of struc-
     tural ambiguity.

3)   A new type of structural relationship is introduced, operating
     between different structural levels in temporal opposition
     (canon).

2)   The various internal repetitions and similarities are non-
     coincident between structural levels and irregular on each level,
     so there are no absolute conditions of opposition in the articula-
     tion on any one level. Nevertheless, the original primary division
     across the bar-line is not lost. It is indicated by Brahms's phrase
     marks, by the texture (the first beat octaves in bar 2 contrasting
     with the surrounding intervals), and by the metrical emphasis.

3)   Through the character of the canonic dux, there are three points
     where the relationship between m1/r1 (-melodic and rhythmic
     structure of top voice) and m2/r2 is strongly articulated — i.e.,
     there are 3 points of non-opposition between different m and r
     structures in tO:

Figure 5

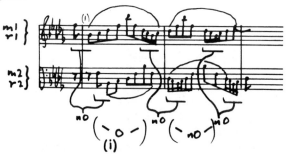

Thus the music is articulated by three structural relationships.
The melodic and rhythmic material of these relationships shows a
distinction between the first two (which are in opposition: see i in

Figure 5) and the second two (which are in non-opposition). The model is therefore:

$$\frac{m/rO:nO}{+O}$$

where the primary division involves conditions of tO, and where the secondary division has only a reinforcing function, coinciding with one of the articulations forming the primary division:

$$\frac{nO:nO:nO}{+O}$$

Variation 6 continues the trends of the earlier models, with its ternary/binary hierarchy, and the elimination of one of the structural levels (h).

Variation 7

This has the simplest kind of model, for there is no secondary division. Brahms writes a simple binary opening:

$$\begin{array}{c} rnO \\ mnO \\ \underline{hnO} \end{array}$$

(The melodic and harmonic levels are not absolutely non-opposed — the fourth beats in each bar are different. This is a minimal distinction within the two bars, however important it is for the whole first phrase.)

Variation 8

For this variation a new level is introduced — h1, which signifies the harmony above the tonic pedal. The harmonic structure of the bass — h2 — and its rhythmic structure — r2 — have been eliminated:

Figure 6

The primary division is again binary, but now the point of division (*) is moved three-quarters of the way through the model. The first division is articulated by three sequential patterns:

Figure 7

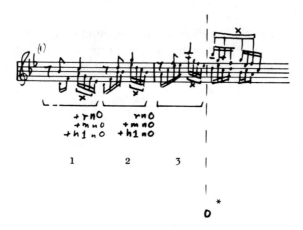

This division (taking in nos. 1, 2 and 3 above) is expressed as:

$$
\begin{aligned}
&+ \text{rnO:} \quad \text{nO} \\
&+ \text{mnO:} + \text{nO} \\
&+ \text{h1nO:} + \text{nO}
\end{aligned}
$$

There is a melodic similarity between this division and the final quarter, as can be seen from the 'x' brackets in Figure 7. After the sequencing in the first division, however, the second has the effect of being an opposition, classed simply as 'O'.

The model of this variation shows a new departure, for the two types of articulation are in tO, that is, they are successive. The first division has a ternary articulation: this whole division then forms the first group of a binary articulation between the first three-quarters and the last quarter of the model:

$$
\begin{aligned}
&\overline{\phantom{+ \text{rnO:} \quad \text{nO:}}} \quad :\text{O} \\
&+ \text{rnO:} \quad \text{nO:} \\
&+ \text{mnO:} + \text{nO:} \\
&+ \text{h1nO:} + \text{nO:}
\end{aligned}
$$

In effect, Brahms has replaced his ambiguous vertical hierarchy by a horizontal one.

With one exception, the subsequent variations do not involve significantly different models. The hierarchical arrangements of the first half of the piece become archetypal for the second half, where Brahms devises more radical ways of generating the articulation. Variation 10 is a good example, where the binary division is weak, but realized through 1) change of mode (major to minor); and 2) discontinuation of the process of octave transposition. As this analysis is not directly concerned with the musical 'content', we move on to the final new kind of articulation.

Variation 15

Two binary divisions operate in tO. The original division at the bar-line is retained, articulated by the harmonic structure:

$$\underline{I - - IV} / \underline{I - - - (V)}$$
$$+ hnO$$

The second division operates between the first idea and an elongation of it:

A model might be:

$$\frac{+ hnO}{+ rnO}$$

though the system is not sophisticated enough to express the proportional relationship between the two divisions. For the present purpose, however, it suffices to note that Brahms uses his normal vertical ambiguity with the unusual juxtaposition of two similar types of articulation (both binary).

CONCLUSIONS

The models fall into certain categories, which will now be tabulated. The preceding analyses show the lines of thought which lead to a cursory description, in the table, of Variations 3, 5, 9–14 and 16–25. Variation 10 is a special case. Although it has a binary division which could be expressed in a model in the manner of those above, its opening 2 bars seem designed to function as an undivided group, as if Brahms were changing the metre of the first half from 4 × 1 bars to 2 × 2 bars. Variation 7 was analyzed as a simple binary structure. But it is not entirely unambiguous, for like the *Aria* it has harmonic tension at the beginning and end but not across the bar-line. More important, Variation 7 marks an important contrast, after the progressive complications up to Variation 6, with a return to the simpler articulation of the *Aria*. For this reason it appears in the table as a return to the *Aria* model.

Table of Transformations

The variation number is followed by category of articulation, arranged in columns of M to M.

i	ii	iii	iv	v	vi
1 M	3 M	7 M	14 M	19 M	22 M
2 *l*	4 *l*	8 BT	15 BB	20 *l*	23 BT
3 M	5 *l*	9 T	16 BB(O)	21 T	24 BT
	6 T(O)	10 –	17 B	22 M	25 M
	7 M	11 *l*	18 B		
		12 BB	19 M		
		13 M			

M : articulation close to the *Aria*

B : binary articulation with a less significant ternary background (i.e., less ambiguously structured than M)

T : ternary articulation with a less significant binary background

l : ternary/binary hierarchy in tnO (the transformation employing an internal repeat: cf. analysis of Variation 2)

BT) or}: horizontal hierarchy, binary/ternary (cf. analysis of Variation 8) or binary/binary BB)

(O) : transformation using tO relationship between structural levels (cf. analysis of Variation 6)

The symbols in the table represent categories of articulation, each one being a summary of the structure. The proportions of the table are determined by a brief departure from the Model in column i, leading to the longest section of deviation over five variations in column iii, and working back to the smaller groupings. Columns i, ii, v and vi are concerned mainly with ternary division: column iv has only binary division. Column iii reflects this structure in reverse, moving from Model to ternary articulation and back again, with a special case (Variation 10) at the centre.

The continuing element is the binary/ternary ambiguity. No variation is entirely free from it, and it is an unmistakable characteristic of at least 19 of them. In addition, the reappearances of the *Aria*'s structure articulate the piece as a whole.

This consideration of the openings does not necessarily reflect the whole music: the arrangement of complete variations may reveal a very different system. But the opening of each variation presumably declares the point of the whole variation, and it is also a place where long-term relationships (especially those referring back to the *Aria*) are strongly felt.

The analysis began by considering each variation separately, with a model of each one. In this summary the model of the *Aria* has been given a special status, and this Model — a model of structure to which each variation is related — may be similar to the 'bass' Brahms mentions in his comments on Variations (see Appendix I). He has little time for simple melodic variation, as the Schubring letter shows, and he praises Beethoven for his beautiful variation of melody, harmony and rhythm. It seems unlikely, in view of his desire to be involved with every level of the structure, that Brahms meant 'bass' literally. It would be hard to show in either Beethoven or Brahms that variation of 'melody, harmony and rhythm' is somehow 'discovered' in the bass-line of the Theme.

In an abstract sense, the models in this analysis might give an answer to this problem. If the articulation of the Theme is retained, the 'meaning' of any variation will be fundamentally the same, however 'ingenious or attractive', as Brahms says, the decorations may be. But by varying the Model of the Theme, while retaining its characteristic ambiguities, he can transform the meaning while maintaining a deep relationship between variations and between them and the Theme: thus he can create something 'new' while making his procedure 'stricter' and 'purer'.

On a practical level, Brahms would be unlikely to think in these terms, if only because they do not help to suggest how the actual material can be manipulated. But the fact that the music can be analyzed in this way, if only in part, suggests that Brahms was successful in his search for a combination of variety and unity.

APPENDIX I

Letter from Brahms to Joachim, June 1856:

(Die Variationen) müssten strenger, reiner gehalten werden. Die Alten behielten durchweg den Bass des Themas, ihr eigentliches Thema streng bei. Bei Beethoven ist die Melodie, Harmonie und der Rhythmus so schön variiert. Ich muss aber manchmal finden, dass Neuere (wir beide!) mehr (ich weiss nicht rechte Ausdrücke) über das Thema wühlen. Wir behalten alle die Melodie ängstlich bei, aber behandeln sie nicht frei, schaffen eigentlich nichts Neues daraus, sondern beladen sie nur...[15]

Variations should surely be kept stricter and purer. Composers used to keep strictly to the bass of the Theme, to their real theme. In Beethoven the melody, harmony and rhythm are so beautifully varied. But I do often find that more recent composers (we two!) wallow more in the Theme (I don't know the right expressions). We all stick anxiously to the melody, but don't treat it freely, really create nothing new out of it, but just weigh it down...

Letter from Brahms to Schubring, February 1869:

Bei einem Thema zu Variationen bedeutet mir eigentlich, fast, beinahe nur der Bass etwas...Variiere ich die Melodie, so kann ich nicht leicht mehr als geistreich oder anmutig sein...Uber den gegebenen Bass erfinde ich wirklich neu, ich erfinde in ihm neue Melodien, ich schaffe...[16]

With a Theme and Variations it is nearly, almost only the bass that really means something for me. If I vary the melody I can't easily be more than ingenious or attractive... Through the given bass I discover truly new things, I discover new melodies in it, I create...

3

Piano Quartet in C Minor, Op. 60, First Movement

INTRODUCTION

The *Piano Quartet in C minor, Op. 60* is often noted in the Brahms literature for its unusual second subject in the first movement. The movement as a whole, however, is an interesting example of typically complex relationships, both in detail and overall structure. In an attempt to convey these two concerns, the following analysis is divided into an examination of the details of the exposition, concentrating mainly on the music leading up to the second subject, and a consideration of the overall tonal structure.

The notion that music includes both detailed and general function is to some extent unrealistic. Though it is a popular distinction, it should be recognized that it begs the questions of how music is formulated and perceived. This conflict can be shown by considering the views of Rosen. He gives an apparently worthwhile caution:

> When there is a correspondence between the detail and the structure, merely to uncover it in the score is insufficient: we must be able to claim that it has always been heard, without being put into words perhaps, but with an effect upon our experience of the musical work.[1]

By using the phrase 'in the score' Rosen clouds the issue, avoiding the normal, more problematic idea of 'in the music'; however, more important is the fact that a musical relationship cannot exist for the analyst until it has been 'heard' or has affected his 'experience' in some way. Showing both the detailed and the overall workings of a movement nevertheless gives a varied approach, reflecting what is probably the varied kind of perception stimulated by music. Some correspondence between detail and structure is in fact revealed in the present study through a similarity of functional characteristics. But no claim is made that an interdependence has been expressed: the isolation of the two is an analytical convenience.

A further problem is the subjectivity involved in describing tonal relationships as sophisticated as those claimed by the second part of our analysis. An objective basis can be found to some extent in an extension of harmonic analysis to tonal relationships. Schoenberg expressed harmonic ambiguity by exposing the conflict between different harmonic functions, without seeking to resolve it in a single analytical metaphor. Sometimes the ambiguity concerns only harmony. For example, functionally equivalent chords might be different in terms of the notes they sound[2]; they are somehow different in effect, but not in their functional harmonic effect. Ambiguity is, however, as much a tonal as a harmonic characteristic: harmonic relationships may express more than one tonality (or, in the spirit of *Structural Functions...*, they may express more than one region related to a tonal centre).

It seems possible to extend Schoenberg's argument so that tonality itself might become ambiguous in function, though this contradicts his description of the tonal centre of a piece. Schoenberg's relating of all chords and regions to a tonal centre can be qualified by the fact that 'tonal centre', though it is crucial to his relationship by regions, is not a definitive concept. This is apparent in his description of what forms a tonality:

> A tonality is expressed by the exclusive use of all its tones. A scale (or part of one) and a certain order of the harmonies affirm it more definitely.[3]

When a tonality is not affirmed, but the music goes on to affirm a second tonality (or region) in a definitive way (by the exclusive use of all its tones, and so on), the conventional idea of tonal structuring does not seem to reflect convincingly the ambiguities of the music. Secondary regions, which are developing expressions of a tonality which was never affirmed, cannot be related in the same way as in conventional tonal structure. This is also a problem with Schenker, whose principle of tonality is summarized by Katz:

> ...tonality...is the expression of one and only one key; there are no modulations outside the key, and these so-called modulatory excursions lie within the tonal orbit.[4]

The problem is to explain how the tonal underlay of 'regions' or 'tonicalization' (in Schenker) is articulated by music as it moves through time. Schenker acknowledges that the opening of a work may be deceptive from this point of view: his example from Beethoven's *First Symphony*[5] highlights the paradox, for the dominant seventh chord 'piled' onto the tonic at the opening is even less likely to be perceived as a kind of tonic chord by the time the strongly opposed, pure tonic does arrive with the first subject theme. The present analysis attempts to recognize these problems, though it does so without being systematic. For example, the background tonal plan for *Op. 60i* in Schenker's system would doubtless begin with a C in the 'Ursatz'. Here it is expressed in diagrams with the tentative opening 'c?'. This cannot claim accuracy, but it draws a contrast between (what Schoenberg calls) the degree of 'affirmation' at the opening and the proper affirmation in the subsequent tonal progression away from the 'tonic'.[6]

The result of this absence of initial affirmation is an unconventional lack of redundant 'confirmation' in the tonal progression.[7] This is as true of the structure itself as it is of the relationship between the structure and historical background. The tonal character of the recapitulation is a 'logical' progression from the exposition and development, but it is quite unconventional for a sonata form, in no way confirming normal tonal expectation.

This last point may go some way to answering a strongly expressed objection to tonal analysis, made by Walker:

> Any analysis which now makes tonality the central issue of a classical symphony, is, in my opinion, slightly dishonest. By the very nature of things tonality is no longer so true for the modern listener whose aural experience is not so vivid as that of his classical counterpart.[8]

Tonality is not a fixed quality 'by the very nature of things', but the greater we assume tonal sensitivity to have been in the past, then the more innovatory a composer's tonal novelties must have been (more, that is, than the 'dishonest' analyst realizes), and presumably the more aware he was of them. What Walker regards as dishonest must be, therefore, not the obvious historical purpose of a tonal analysis, but any implicit claim that it is generated by authentic tonal sensitivity, aside from the question of relevance for the listener. As Schoenberg demonstrates in *Brahms the Progressive*[9], the only claim is a comparative one: the tonal argument rests on an appeal to specific examples, or in this case to tonal convention.

ANALYSIS

A 2-bar introduction is followed by an 8-bar melody for V1., accompanied homophonically (with some syncopation) by Vla. and Vlc. The melody is built from a semitone motive, announced twice in the 2-bar antecedent, developed in a 4-bar consequent, and extended to form a 2-bar cadential group:

Piano Quartet in C Minor

Figure 1

The 2 + 8 division of this first phrase (phrase 1) is shown by the harmonic progression:

$$
\begin{array}{lll}
1-2 & 3 & \qquad\qquad - \qquad\qquad (8)-9/10 \\
\text{c:} \quad \text{I(?)} & \text{I} & (-V-I-V\ldots\ldots\text{VI})- \quad V \\
\hline
\multicolumn{3}{c}{2+8}
\end{array}
$$

which is articulated by the instrumental opposition between 1–2 and 3–10 (Pf./Strings).

The similarity of the opening and closing pairs of bars:

$$\underline{1\ 2}\ 3\ 4\ 5\ 6\ 7\ 8\ \underline{9\ 10}$$

suggests a symmetrical organization which is also evident in the motivic grouping:

Figure 2

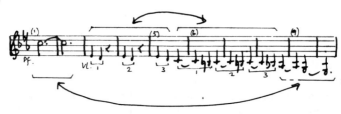

The bass line turns around the same axis of symmetrical division:

Figure 3

The opening phrase, therefore, has a complex articulation which mixes conventional and symmetrical division:

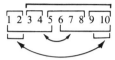

Phrase 2 (11–20) begins on the flat seventh degree of C. A 2-bar introduction is followed by a development of the melody from phrase 1. Its antecedent is extended to 4 bars, with each second bar (14 and 16) inverting the V1. and V1c. parts from 13 and 15. The melodic line now moves in two directions, with the downward progression covering a sixth (from phrase 1, Figure 4i) preceded by an upward sixth (Figure 4ii), filled in at the octave by Bflat in the first upbeat bar (14):

Figure 4

The motivic organization of phrase 1 is developed from 3 + 4 pairs of notes to 4 + 5:

Figure 5

The sequential development in phrase 2 fills 8 bars, before arriving at the 2-bar cadence material which closed phrase 1. In phrase 1 the closing bars form an imperfect cadence (8^3–10). In phrase 2 this dominant close (now in Bflat) is elided into the final bar of the melody (20^{2-3}), followed by a G major chord (21). Although this repeats the implied chord of the 2-bar cadence in phrase 1, it is a distant progression from an imperfect cadence in Bflat at the close of phrase 2. An interchange of harmonies related more to C or Bflat continues through the next 8 bars:

```
        21  22   23   24  25   26   27
     c: V  (chromatic)   IV   H̶   V
  bflat:V̶I̶       VI   I    V   (H̶H̶?  V̶I̶)
```

These chromatic progressions are reflected at the melodic level by more extended forms of the semitone motive:

Figure 6

Both the harmonic rhythm of 21–8, and the return of G at the seventh bar (27) to form a cadence in C, articulate an 8-bar phrase. Over a 3-bar upbeat (29–31), E (pizz.) then leads to the dominant seventh (F,31), which resolves on Eflat, the first note of the main theme. The prominent E's in the extended upbeat to phrase 4 seem to evolve from the chromatic progression in 21–5. The imperfect cadence in C (26–7) interrupts a downward sequence, but the continuation would have moved to E in the bass:

Figure 7

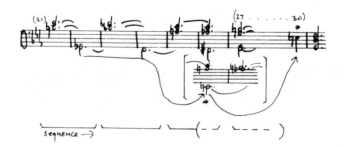

A review of these opening phrases shows that the function of the extended series of ambiguous chords from 21-7 is to integrate the harmony of an early sequential development in phrase 2. A progression in C from tonic to dominant has an embedded sequential development on the seventh degree:

Figure 8

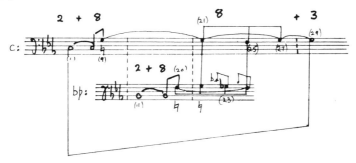

The convenient division of 1–31 into phrases 1, 2 and 3 must be qualified by the close relationship of phrases 2 and 3. Two introductory bars (1–2) precede an 8-bar period.[10] The same introduction on Bflat is then followed by a development of 3–4 (13–4), a 2-bar varied repetition (15–6), a 4-bar development (17–20, based on 5–8), and an 8-bar liquidation,[11] where characteristic features are generally eliminated into 2 closing bars of static dominant harmony (in C, 27–8²). The harmonic scheme of Figure 8 is therefore articulated:

2	+	8	2	+	16		3	+	(phrase 4)
intro.		period	intro.		sentence		intro.		

The quiet ending of this section is interrupted by the string Aflat and downward scale in 31: Aflat is texturally and dynamically forced, and prominent through the absence of small-scale voice-leading to prepare it. This emphasis launches it from its immediate context to add another step to the progression of *forte* notes so far:

Figure 9

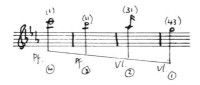

Through this stepwise movement, 31 continues the introductory function of
the previous opening groups, leading into the first subject theme, phrase 4.

Phrase 4 follows the pattern of irregular phrasing; like phrases 1 and 2
it covers 10 bars (32–41). It also imitates the melodic structure of 3–9: two
repeated motives followed by a downward progression covering a sixth (in
the Pf.):

Figure 10

The antecedent and consequent are now more separated, in contrast to their
motivic overlap in phrase 1 (see Figures 1 and 5). Taken together, the Pf.
and Vl. parts show a development from the semitone motive:

Figure 11

The cadence is extended from 2 to 4 bars (38–41). Brahms avoids the brak-
ing effect of short closing groups, but extends the cadence within the phrase
(in contrast to phrase 2, where the cadence became detached and extended
as the second section of a sentence):

The relative independence of consequent from antecedent in conjunction
with an extended closing group relates phrase 4 to phrase 2:

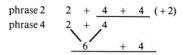

The suggestion in phrase 4 of more regular articulation and a more flowing sequence of phrases is confirmed by phrase 5 (42–51), which has no introduction, and which begins with the first clear-cut 8-bar phrase. The strong division into 4 + 4 at 46 is created by a modulation involving the chromatic change of Aflat (44) to A (46), the sounding of all instruments on the first beat, the tonal development of the 4 consequent bars (46–9) and the accelerated pace of the strings (2 + 2/1 + 1 + 1 + 1).

A 4 + 4 division is repeated in phrases 6 (52–9) and 7 (60–9); the increased regularity within each phrase is matched by an overall symmetrical relationship at the end of the first subject section:

```
phrase 5   8  +  2
phrase 6      8*
phrase 7   8* +  2
```

This passage includes the first succession of unambiguous 8-bar phrases (marked * above). Consecutive 8-bar phrases in 13–28 were hidden by an introductory pair of bars and an ambiguous area across the division:

```
11................19  20  21  22  23.....
2      +      8       +2?
      10?              8        +    (etc.)
```

A general division of the first 70 bars can be identified at 32:

```
phrases 1–3            phrases 4–7

c?          G   /  c    (g)    Bflat /  Eflat
↑  bflat    ↑
period ↑    upbeat
    sentence

introduction   /  first subject   /  second subject.....
```

However, there are as many features which give an overall continuity to this section as features which give conventional sonata divisions. This is especially evident in the relationship between phrases 1 and 4.

Phrase 1 is marked off by the forceful process of repetition (in the form of sequential development): it is therefore clearly articulated at both ends. Phrase 4, on the other hand, has an extended dominant preparation (phrase 3, upbeat): and although phrase 5 brings in new melodic material and rhythmic pattern (41/2), the articulation between phrases 4 and 5 is the weakest such division so far. Phrase 1, therefore, has the characteristics of the beginning of a fragmented introduction, and phrase 4 of the beginning of a substantial continuous section.

But phrase 4 does not clarify the ambiguities of phrase 1. For example, the melodic progression of a sixth from 3–9 is already completed to an octave progression across phrases 2 and 3:

Figure 12

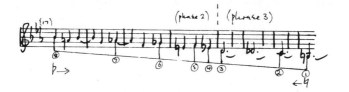

This prefigures the same type of progression in phrase 4, completed in the consequent groups and copying the chromatic alteration of the lower octave:

Figure 13

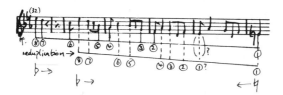

Phrase 4 is distinguished from the first three harmonically, with its I–V progression resolving on I at the beginning of phrase 5 (42). But the harmony of the introduction predicts that such simple relationships will be followed by distant progression (taking I–V/VII, 1–11, as a model). The harmony of phrase 4, however, does not move into a distant progression until the end of phrase 5 (49), suggesting an extension of the time-scale of harmonically ambiguous progression, rather than the establishment of simple functional relationships after a roving introduction.

The tonality gives no more clarification. Although there is a local confirmation of C minor by phrase 4, the effect of the first 70 bars as a whole is tonally unstable. As will be discussed below, the traditional role of the first subject in establishing a tonal centre for the movement is missing: so is the traditional formal relationship between introduction and first subject where the first subject clarifies the tonality of the introduction.

The conflicting features which make for formal ambiguity can be summarized in opposing groups:

A) *Division into introduction/first subject*

   —repeating harmonic structure (c–bflat–G/c–g–Bflat)
   —rhythmic patterns articulating long sections (♩/♪♪♪)
   —dynamic opposition (p–pp/f–ff)

B) *Features not characteristic of this division*

   —sequential development in introduction in distant harmonic relationship (phase 2)
   —lack of distinct first subject theme (phrase 4 is a development of phrases 1 and 2)
   —tonality obscure in both introduction and first subject
   —irregular phrasing continues past first subject theme

The rhythmic patterning and regularization of phrasing mentioned above prepare for the second subject section, with its string of 8-bar phrases in groups of continuous rhythmic pattern (quavers, 70–85/triplet quavers, 86–101/quavers, 102–9). The motivic organization of the introduction and first subject section also evolves towards the second subject.

The fourth, Eflat–Bflat, which announces the downward arpeggio figure prominent in the second subject section, is already a significant motive in the opening phrases. In 3 it is a counterpoint to the second, Eflat–D (C–F, V1c.). The two intervals are used in invertible counterpoint in *13–16* (V1. and V1c.), with the fourth transposed to its second subject pitch (Bflat–Eflat, V1c. 13: cf. Pf. 70) by the motivically generated harmonic step down a tone between 1 and 11. The fourth continues at this stage to depend on various settings of the second. For example, its identity between B and E from 28 to 30 (B in the sustained lower parts, E pizz.) results from the anticipation of F in 31 (Pf.) by a leading note (see Pf. 30–1), creating the vivid attraction of a semitone between E and F. The fourth progression of Figure 9 is similarly dependent on the relationship between two seconds, C–Bflat (1–11) and Aflat–G (31–43). This hierarchy persists until the fusion of introduction and first subject is completed by phrase 4.

The second then loses its formative significance; no longer shaping the harmony, it becomes decorative, figuring the movement in thirds of the strings from 42 to 55. As the regularization of the phrasing prepares for the second subject, the fourth becomes prominent. In phrase 5 it is given in a direct form in the Pf., with a first beat accent in the final notes (Figure 14i) stressing the range of a fourth: the primary interval (the second) has so far been accented on its first note, which in this setting (shown by the asterisks) is always on the weakest beat with a passing harmony. In phrase 6 a melodic figure anticipates the rhythm and direction of the beginning of the second subject theme, covering a fourth on its first appearance (Figure 14ii); and in the second half of this phrase V1. and V1c. use the semitone and tone to decorate fourths (Figure 14iii: cf. decorated thirds, 42–8). In phrase 7 the fourth appears as a discrete motive: the two halves of the phrase show that the fourth has changed status from a resultant interval to an alternative to the semitone, with the fourth in the strong position in the antecedent (Figure 14iv):

Figure 14

The primary interval at the opening is also active at a harmonic and tonal level: the connection between these different levels is initiated by one idea of functional ambiguity. The progression C–Bflat from 1 to 11 is the first step of a melodic progression linking introduction and first subject (see

Figure 9), and also a movement of the bass which sets off the sequential development of the introduction (see Figure 8). The levels then divide into a more elaborate texture, not to converge until the end of the development section.

The melody and the bass-line of the first two phrases have similar characteristics, moving mainly by conjunct motion, sometimes by fourths. In phrase 1, both melody and bass have a range of a sixth (cf. Figures 3 and 4). Phrase 3 includes two bars of an arpeggio figure in the bass (21, 23) and phrase 4 has a tonic pedal. As the fourth evolves in the motivic structure of the melody the bass-line takes on a different character, based on the arpeggio figure from phrase 3:

Figure 15

The arpeggio figure naturally includes fourths and fifths. This evolution in the bass matches the tonal progression, where C has moved to its relative major, Eflat, through the two progressions C–Bflat and Bflat–Eflat, with intervening confirmations of a local tonic (G–c–g):

phrase motive	1	2	3	4	5	6	7
		2nd				4th	

bass	conjunct			pedal	arpeggio	

harmony/ tonality	on c			on Bflat	

In contrast to this homogeneous structure, the progression of phrasing and tonality through the introduction and first subject section arrives, in the second subject, at a state of conflict. The tonality in the second subject is in a tense condition, the degree of establishment being out of step with the tonal relationship:

	introduction/first subject	*second subject*
key:	tonic	second region (must resolve)
degree of establishment:	unconfirmed	stable

With its 8-bar divisions, however, the second subject brings a proportional stability. The articulatory process on the level of phrasing is played out by the end of the exposition. A recycling of this process helps to define the major divisions of the sonata form, which is contradicted in an overall sense by the tonality (though the tonal planes are mostly confined by normal sonata divisions: see below). The development section begins again with irregular phrasing:

$$\underset{122}{4+4+4+8+\underline{6+6}+\underline{6+4}+\underline{6+6}+\underline{8+6+6}}\ \underset{196}{(+3)}$$

leading through a distorted first subject recapitulation:

$$\underset{196}{10+7}+\underset{227}{\underline{4+10+9}}$$

to return to regular 8-bar divisions in the recapitulation second subject section (which includes one new extension, to 10 bars — 260-9).

A review of the exposition shows that, while working within a conventional framework, Brahms continually frustrates conventional expectations. For example, according to one writer the introduction fits the conventional expectations of sonata form, even in the detail of a unison opening:

> The essential aesthetic of the Classic sonata-form introduction is a statement of the tonic, often in a bare unison, and then a departure from the key with a return, usually on the dominant, preparing the tonic of the exposition.[12]

But Brahms's 'departure' in the introduction takes an unconventional form: a sequential development as early as the second phrase puts an emphasis on the opening material and proportioning which tends to reduce any definitiveness about the main theme. Similarly, the 'return' is effected through a string of chromatically related chords, creating a tonal ambiguity which only a firm tonic could counteract. But the 'tonic of the exposition' is only a fleeting reference, the subsequent remote progression reducing its ability to give the first subject section an unequivocal tonal centre.[13]

Although the modulation to Eflat for the second subject is conventional, once again the manipulation of material turns out to be unorthodox. The series of character variations which follows the second subject theme is a unique example of its kind. Brahms sets up the expectation of a contrast between the first and second subject sections, if only through the opposition of a solo string opening (3–10 etc.) and the solo piano second subject theme.

Typically, it is an extreme contrast in the overall form, with a set of variations halting the developmental structure of the introduction and first subject.[14]

In the development section, which is introduced by a change to the minor mode of Eflat, five phrases give dramatic transformations of first subject material, leading through a long, descending sequence:

B: I-V / A: I-H / roving / G: I-V / F: I-H
142   148   154   164   170

The two sequential groups include references to the harmonic pattern of the introduction:

	I	V / VII	V
Exposition:	1	9 11	21/7
Development:	142(B)	147 148	151 (-I,152)
Development:	164(G)	169 170	173 (-I,174)

G arrives in the bass at 176, to remain as a pedal and then the goal of each cadence until the recapitulation second subject:

Figure 16

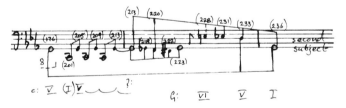

The function of the insistent G is explained by an exact repetition in 217–26 of phrase 3 from the exposition. This is the only phrase from the first 69 bars to be recapitulated exactly, stressing the recall of its original tonal function. In the exposition it was a dominant cadence. It cannot have this local function in the recapitulation, surrounded by tonality on or in G; but by association it can reinforce the function of a long section on G in the movement as a whole:

I(c?)   V(G)   I
1etc.   313

The first section over G (176–196) is a local dominant, which crescendos into the brief appearance of C opening the recapitulation (201–13). The new resolution to phrase 3 (227 et seq) then establishes G as a tonic. But this division of function is obscured by the stability of G before it is firmly established. The development section has precedents for the forceful interpretation of dominant harmonies as tonic regions (141–2 and 161–4). And the highlighted G's in 196–7 are associated with the first 2 bars of the movement: here at the emotional climax of the movement the very first gesture of a tonic is recalled. The next phrase, the opening of the recapitulation, takes from the exposition phrase 1 rather than phrase 4 as its model, the phrase which had its cadence on G (cf. 9–10 and 205, as well as 209 and 213) where the status of C as a tonic was not confirmed by the following harmony. Equally threatening to C in the recapitulation is the variation of phrase 6 which now appears on G (213–6): the dominant is associated, only 15 bars into the recapitulation, with a phrase which in the exposition was already a long way from the first (undefined) tonal centre. In the radical development of sonata form convention, Brahms introduces, at the end of the development section, characteristics of a new tonal region which will occupy most of the recapitulation. By bringing the same kind of ambiguity into the first subject recapitulation as was used in the introduction (which was as strongly a 'first subject' as the apparent first subject theme) he avoids any definitive confirmation of the tonic in the recapitulation.

The surface features identifying the movement's I–V–I progression are at three points where the normal dense texture is replaced by one pitch. The first is at the beginning, where Pf. octaves on C are isolated by dynamics and instrumental contrast. The following Bflat, isolated in the same way (11), assimilates this feature into the musical structure through its motivic and implied harmonic relationships. As the progression fades into the general structure, each step becoming more integrated (see Figure 9), the strength of the opening remains as a long-term effect. The second feature, the G's in 196–7, is followed by a return to C at the end of the movement, with bare octaves in 313–4.[15] The two C's (1 and 313) are isolated, not only texturally, but by their rhythmic stasis. The G's are more integrated, by triplet figuration and by their resolution of the preceding chromatic progression in the bass (over a G pedal). This resolution at the octave, however, confirms the significance of both the octave interval (cf. 1–2, 28–30, 78–81, 120–5) and the octave range (cf. arpeggio figure, Figures 12 and 13). The closing phrase of the movement stresses the octave, setting a final version of the first subject with octave figures and octave displacements:

Figure 17

The octave markers relating the I–V–I harmonic base of the movement do not coincide with the tonal progression:

c? – Eflat – G – C-c

which threatens the balance of the movement in relation to sonata form proportions:

c?	–	Eflat	–	G	–	C-c
exposition		development	recap.			coda

This threat is modal as well as proportional, for the arpeggio progression of the tonal structure is first resolved by C major:

Eflat – G – C
70 (176)236 288

The octave markers are significant, therefore, not only in counteracting the proportional weakness of the introduction and coda (the tonic minor sections), but also in identifying the minor (313) rather than the major (288) resolution.[16] Thus the two progressions are not synchronized:

	1	176		313
I(c)		V		I
c?	Eflat	G	C	
1/32	70	236	288	

The separation of the major and minor resolutions is achieved by a 'second development' leading away from C and back to a G pedal (292–303). Both resolutions give the end of the movement an emphasis which in an archetypal sonata form would be fulfilled by the tonic return of the recapitulation.

To sum up, such a structure relies on the possibility of ambiguity of tonal function and definition. The recapitulation G operates at two levels, before 196 as a dominant, after 236 as a new tonal region, with the distinction obscured between these points. Eflat has an equivalent status to the G (established as a new region) because it is established as much through indirect as direct progression (see the move to Bflat in phrase 5). Finally, the whole tonal complex is bound up with the unconventional setting of the second subject. The necessary planes of static tonality could have been achieved with or without variation form, but the coordination of the tonal character of the movement with the tonal demands of variation form gives the music a thorough logic.

APPENDIX II

There is no commonly known precedent for Brahms's use of a Theme and Variations in the second subject of *Op. 60i*. The first movement of Schubert's *Piano Sonata in C minor,* however, shows a similar procedure.

Schubert's second subject section comprises a theme (39–53), a simple variation (53–67), a second variation extended by 4 bars and in the minor mode (67–85), and a closing passage (85–98, to be called a 'coda'). The recapitulation of this section is a regular transposition, whereas Brahms adds new variations to his set in the recapitulation. Though such an explicit Theme and Variations second subject as in the Brahms is probably unique, Schubert seems to have been developing a trend. The Sonatas in a(1817), a(1825), D and C all have a simple variation of their second subject theme within the section: in the *C minor Sonata* the variation principle is used more exclusively, though the length of the theme makes it a less recognizable kind of organization than in the Brahms.

This connection between the two movements is one of many correspondences. The two second subject themes have similar opening ideas:

Figure 18

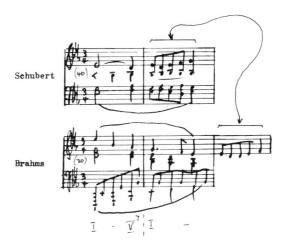

In addition, Schubert's theme seems to have influenced Brahms outside the second subject area. The most significant harmonic event in the Sonata's second subject is the sudden remote progression from an Eflat7 chord to Dflat7 in 48. There is no parallel in Brahms's second subject, but there is at the opening, with a drop from C (1) to Bflat (11). These two progressions have a comparable prominence, and the same harmonic setting. In both, the rogue harmony extends a I–V progression (the dominant being Bflat in Schubert–50, and G in Brahms–21/7).

The opening of the Sonata is well known for being based on the theme of Beethoven's *32 Variations on an Original Theme, in C minor, WoO 80.* In modelling his first subject so closely on the Beethoven, Schubert was using an earlier background, one which became a recurrent concern for Brahms. The common melodic and harmonic progression of the two is presented in a classic rhythmic pattern, that of the Sarabande/Chaconne. The archetypal, for example Handelian, version of this is:

Beethoven adapts it thus:

Figure 19

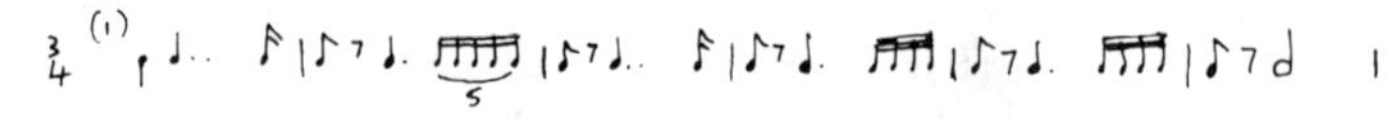

and Schubert removes some of Beethoven's second-beat stress:

Figure 20

This kind of rhythmic pattern is also typical of the introduction, first subject and development section of Brahms's first movement. In the exposition it reflects Schubert's down-beat stress, and there are textural similarities in the piano part (cf. Schubert's opening and Brahms–32 et seq). In the development section Brahms adds the characteristic final semiquaver of Schubert's pattern:

Figure 21

This rhythmic characteristic is largely absent from the second subject in both Schubert and Brahms, its influence restricted to a gently stressed second beat (e.g. Schubert, 48–50 and Brahms, 78–81). But in both it makes an appearance in the coda, for two bars in the Sonata (86–7) and in Brahms as a more distinct reference to the main theme (110–8): in both it introduces the submediant minor chord (Aflat minor).

Thus Brahms follows Schubert in the formal settings of this rhythmic pattern. It is the principal rhythm of the first subject. It plays an important part in the development section. And it rounds off the second subject, though it is only hinted at in the Theme and Variations.

A second rhythm common to both movements is less sharply characterized, and not confined to any formal position. Schubert first interrupts the Sarabande rhythm in 7 (discounting the decorative upbeat to 4), with a three-quaver upbeat to the next bar. Brahms comes close to this:

Figure 22

Both movements then break into more or less continuous semiquavers in one part or another, running up to the second subject. Both take the upbeat rhythm into the Variations, and in both it plays a primary and a secondary role. In Schubert it acts primarily as a lead into each subdivision of the section — theme, Variation 1, Variation 2 and coda — but in Variation 2 its relationship to the bar-line is altered to make it an 'upbeat' to the third beat (78, 81–4). In Brahms it acts characteristically as an upbeat to the third beat (82, 88–9, 96–7); but in the coda it returns to its original position (111–2, 115–6, though the third quaver here is a phrase-end rather than an upbeat).

Apart from the procedural connection between the second subject sections, these correspondences are very much on the surface of each movement. Thanks to Brahms's extensive developmental processes (which he suspends only in the second subject, and even there not in the sense that melodic variation, with new variations in the 'recapitulation', is developmental) the influence of the Sonata cannot be very deep within a section. But Brahms does reveal his model at those points where he must proceed as Schubert did, that is, at the major points of articulation in the sonata form. An example comes at the end of the development section. To lead to the reappearance of his first subject, Schubert uses an 8-bar bass-line ascending chromatically from the dominant note to the tonic (152–9 + 160). Brahms uses the same idea at the same point in his structure (176–190), with an ascending chromatic bass, underpinned by a dominant pedal and extended over 9 bars to lead up to Aflat.

There are many other similarities between the movements — prominent degrees of the scale (especially the submediant note, Aflat), cadential mannerisms (cf. Schubert, 96^3–8 and Brahms, 210^3–2), and the kind of motivic relationships which invariably bind Brahms to his Viennese models. But these connections are only to be expected if Brahms was modelling at a more fundamental level, in one section, on the Schubert.

Brahms would certainly know of the Beethoven–Schubert connection mentioned above. He would study the Schubert, perhaps to see how Schubert used a variation theme in a sonata form. It turns out that variation procedure was taken into the second subject: having noticed this, Brahms would typically want to try an extreme version of the same principle.

4

Symphony No. 4 in E Minor, Op. 98, First Movement

INTRODUCTION

The following analysis of the first movement of the *Symphony in E minor, Op. 98* uses terms which are conventional and mostly traditional. However, the discussion of music of a symphonic scale, with its elaborate figurations and reduplication, often leads to drastic diagrammatic reduction (see, for example, Figure 16). To some extent this follows the conventions of Schenkerian analysis, but it is not systematically derivative. Various considerations influence the reduction to contrapuntal backgrounds, and it is hoped that they will be self-explanatory where they are not discussed in the text.

The analysis discovers, early in the movement, an unconventional procedural conflict. Brahms abandons the process in the final coda, so that though this music is interesting from other points of view, it is not discussed here.

ANALYSIS

The first section of 18 bars is marked off by a varied restatement of the first theme (from 18^4): this section will be called the first period. A casual division of this period shows a shortening of the phrase lengths:

$$8 + 4 + 2 + 2 + 2$$

Along with this, a tendency for the opening phrases to be articulated in units of 1 bar gives way to smaller units of articulation as the phrase contracts. The detailed articulation towards the end of the period is related to the proportions of the phrasing, explicitly in 13–14, and less so in 15–18:

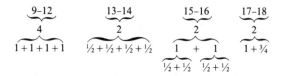

Thus the music accelerates towards the end of the period. It does so over an irregular number of bars (10, bars 9–18) which follow the 8-bar first theme.

Whereas the phrasing of the whole period contracts, this 8-bar melody was generated through a regular sequential process. In its first four notes there is no overt melodic pattern:

Figure 1

but the rhythmic framework, dividing the notes into two intervals moving in opposite directions, sets up a binary association:

Figure 2

This becomes the model for a similar relationship covering 4 bars, generated by melodic sequence:

Figure 3

The process of expansion continues. These 4 bars generate another 4, which similarly divide into 2 bars plus a tone-down sequence. More complex relationships are being set up, but basically 5-8 stand in the same sequential relationship to 1-4 as 3-4 do to 1-2, and as 2 does to 1:

Figure 4

This is the limit of the process. The first 8 bars are therefore divided off in our analysis and called the 'first theme', even though there is a continuous melody over the first 18 bars. The first theme is followed, not by an 8-bar consequent, but by 10 bars. The first 4 of these have the effect of prolongation rather than consequence, though their function after the theme is ambiguous. Bars 9–12 interrupt the melodic progression of 1–8. They stop the first theme abruptly with a decorated C, which covers 4 bars. But until the third beat of 9 a succession rather than a contrast is suggested, that is, a conventional phrase extension:

Figure 5

This simple ambiguity is a symptom of the dualistic nature of the first period. It contains the kind of asymmetries (cf. Figure 27) and contrasts which can develop and resolve in a sonata structure. Yet it begins with a gesture of rigidity—an impressively regular 8-bar melodic progression, with the suggestion of a developmental extension, as Figure 5 suggests, but which is overtly closed off by the prolongation.

Though there is a contrast between the first theme and the following 10 bars, the forward drive of the irregular period begins in the first theme itself.

The rhythm is mechanistic, as is the generative principle of the notes:

Figure 6[1]

set 1   set 2

Equally mechanistic is the directional pattern of the 2-note cells (╲ and ╱). The generation of the actual melody is not so. By repeating a note and thus substituting an octave (x) for the initial third (y) Brahms strengthens the 4 + 4 articulation, and in effect reverses the order of intervals:

‖: small (third) – large (sixth) :‖   ‖: large (octave⁰) – small (third) :‖

This reversal reinforces the closed, symmetrical aspect of the phrase. But the whole period is proportioned by the resolution of progressions initiated in the first theme. They begin with an interruption of the principle which generated the first 4 bars, that is, with the octave duplication.

We can now examine how the first theme provides the impetus for an extended period, while giving the impression of being closed. The dualism in the two 'halves' of period 1 arises from the first theme itself.

The movement in the upper part — B/C — is immediately resolved by a return to B:

Figure 7

giving 1–4 a closed sense (along with the I–IV–V–I harmony). And progression 'b' (above) reduplicates this progression in inversion, resolving on to the first beat of the internal consequent (5–8), reinforcing the 4 + 4 articulation. It acts so strongly in this way because it comes half a bar early:

Figure 8

(cf. an extension of completion, Figure 27)

Meanwhile 'E' sounds in the higher register ('x' in Figure 7), beginning a new progression:

Figure 9

It is emphasized with a dynamic indication, implying a subtle prominence for the new, high register (x).

The melody now reaches a melodic stasis of 4 bars (C^1–C^2–C^1–C^2) which delays the course of this progression. The middle register C ('y' above) resolves on the third beat of 17: the high register progression drops briefly onto B at 17^4 (Oboe) but is resolved convincingly only by the B which begins the first theme restatement (18^4). Meanwhile the middle part resolves downwards (as shown in Figure 10), with the first stepwise melodic motion; this is a new idea acting as a consequent to the prolongation (9–18 = 9–12/13–18) but fulfilling the tendencies of the first theme (y):

Figure 10

The 'closed' quality of bars 13–16 is evident from this — they contain a contracted reduplication ('y') of progression 'x'. If 9–12 are considered a prolongation of the first theme, then 13–16 stand out as the effective consequent to the first 12 bars. They mark the strongest contrast, using a diminution of the first period's background (y > x). The register of this consequent
confirms its contrasting function, for it completes the lower register progression ('y') while the upper is suspended ('z').

Looking on, it seems that the octave figuration of the restated first
theme:

Figure 11

is derived from the octave separation in period 1:

Figure 12

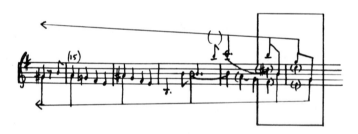

But the first theme has influenced more than the melodic dimension of
the prolongation and consequent. The background pairs of thirds in Figure
6 are chromatically related. Set 1 contradicts set 2 by the alteration of:

Figure 13

This downward motion results from the melodic sequence in 5–8 (cf. Figure
5).

The implication of this is made explicit in the prolongation. The harmony is now enriched by a chromatic bass:

Figure 14

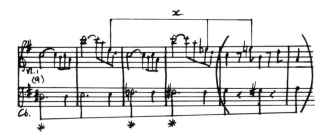

This takes in three of the notes given in Figure 13 (marked *, Figure 14), and the melodic figuration involves an enharmonic version of D–Dsharp (D–Eflat, cf. 'x' above and Figure 7). The completion of the bass-line (Figure 14) up to the dominant note is transferred in the consequent to a higher voice, though the bass sounds a final B:

Figure 15

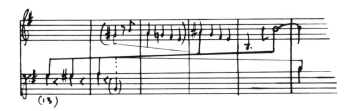

There is a strong contrast between this rising progression and the general 'fall' of the first theme. This is the effect as the bass-line moves into the open in the prolongation. But it began as a counterpoint to the whole melodic progression of Figure 10. It started at the same time, and its octave (and fifteenth) displacement is resolved at the equivalent place, in the final cadence of the period.

Assembling these progressions gives a picture of the melodic structure from 5 to 18, with its closed incipit (1–4):

Figure 16

The sections of prolongation and consequent are now seen as sections of different contrapuntal character.[2] Bracket 'x' in Figure 16 (the prolongation) is a bare, oblique movement of chromatic steps against pedal; 'y' is more complex, with 4 moving parts (i, ii, iii and iv above): but it refers doubly to the first theme, first by the explicit scale completion (i), second by referring, in conjunction with bracket 'z', to the opening counterpoint:

Figure 17 (cf. Figure 16)

And 'z' is strongly characterized by sounding the dominant (B) in every relevant octave.

The restatement of the first theme covers 18^4–26. It is changed in two important ways:

1. The woodwind no longer shadows the string melody in syncopated crochets. In the 4-bar antecedent (18^4–22), together with the viola, it makes the background of Figure 6 more explicit, arranging it thus:

Figure 18

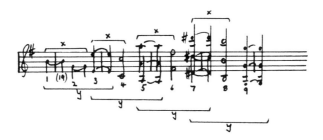

Each combination of instruments:

1-2-3, Vla/ 3-4-5, Cl and Fg/ 5-6-7, Ob and Vl/ 7-8-9, Fl, Cl and Fg

begins on the upbeat, reinforcing the two-note cells of the model ('x' above), and each group overlaps the following cell, producing downward triadic forms ('y'). This progression is figured in tetrachords:

Figure 19

derived from the first period consequent:

Figure 20

The connection between these two is clearly heard as the viola takes over the melody notes in the same octave:

Figure 21

In the 4-bar consequent, the woodwind progression turns into a real counterpoint to the theme:

Figure 22

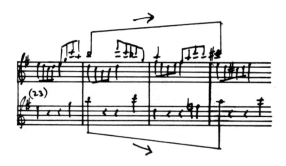

2. Substituted for the original tonic pedal in the bass (1–4) is the original woodwind syncopated part, inverted into the bass, a twelfth down:

Figure 23

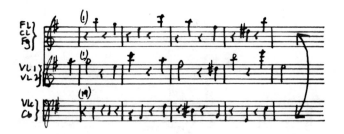

The bass reverts to its original notes for the consequent (23–6) figured by familiar octave duplications, imitating the direction of the melody:

Figure 24

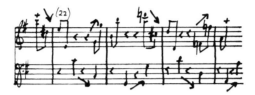

There is an increasing contrapuntal complexity: the antecedent is given a new bass-line (Figure 23), the consequent a new counter-melody (Figure 22). The antecedent uses figures from period 1's consequent, and in the 4-bar consequent here (23–6) a new harmonic richness is introduced, with the kind of chromatic relationship originally set up between antecedent and consequent of the first theme (see Figure 13):

Figure 25

In the expected 4-bar prolongation (27–30) the original contrapuntal design is at first confirmed by a moving part against a static part. But at the third bar (29) the static part begins to move:

Figure 26

The bass-line generates a much longer structure than at the opening. In period 1, the first theme and prolongation were considered to be both contrasted and successive. The bass-line crossed the division between these two groups with a sequential pattern. This involved a tonic note with two functions; overtly, it marked the first movement of the long chromatic bass-line (contrast), but it also acted as a completion of the sequential pattern which began in bar 5 (succession):

Figure 27

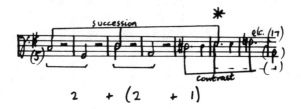

In the second period prolongation, this succession is missing:

Figure 28

The delayed 'E' in Figure 27 (*) created the first irregular growth (in relation to regular, 4-bar phrasing), the first impetus to the extension of period 1 (16 to 18 bars). 'E' is expected on the first beat of 9 (see Figure 27), but it is delayed, so the effect of the sequencing (2 + 2, etc.) is carried over an extra bar (2 + [2 + 1], etc.). The delaying power of the changing note Dsharp (27) in Figure 28 generates an even more expansive structure. Considering the basic direction of the counterpoint in Figure 26, the prolongation holds the upper part:

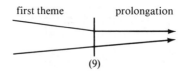

whereas in period 2 it moves in contrary motion:

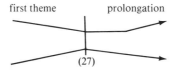

So it cannot be resolved as stably as in period 1 within the same time-scale.

After the restatement of the first theme there are two 6-bar groups (27–32, 33–38), each closing with a synthesis of elements of bars 13–18. What was originally a succession is now performed simultaneously:

	consequent figures		tetrachords		dominant 8°s
period 1	2	+	2	+	2
	(13–14)		(15–16)		(17–18)
period 2			consequent figures		
			tetrachord		
			dominant pedal		
			2		
			(31–2)		

The original melodic line can be split up to produce the new 3-part complex:

Figure 29

Through the varied repetition 33–8 = 27–32, the prolongation changes its function. It now acts as an antecedent:

Figure 30

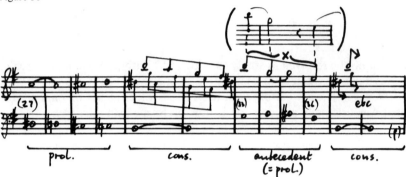

This is demonstrated diagrammatically to bring out the melodic background of 33–36. This second variation of the melody of the prolongation (x) is generated by thirds descending from B, anacrusis (represented here by syncopation), and octave transposition (see bars 33–6), all elements of the first theme. This relationship to the first theme (see 'x' above) reinforces its antecedent character.

The combination of material with first theme associations continues into the consequent. It is contracted from 6 bars (13–18) to 2 bars (31–2 and 37–8), and the dominant pedal is removed as it is transposed up a fourth:

Figure 31

The tetrachord descending from E was the major progression in period 1 (compare 'x' above with 'z' in Figure 10).

The extension of this tetrachord through a 6-bar phrase (39–45[1]) reflects the transitional tonal progression. The melodic progression overshoots its original tendency towards octave completion. In period 1 the octave lines (Figure 16 (i), (ii) and (iii)) polarized the voice-leading around the dominant and tonic. Now the progression goes to the dominant leading note, which is reinforced by repetition:

Figure 32

This passage creates perhaps the greatest excitement so far. Both melody and harmony suddenly move in crotchets, for the first time. The bass-line once more adopts a pedal, figured by octave leaps in crotchets ('x' above), an energetic diminution of the melodic contour in 9–12 (the original prolongation). This and the preceding phrase seem to begin to close the whole section, with a hint of symmetry in material and articulation:

$$
\begin{array}{cccccccc}
4 & + & 2 & + & 2 & + & 4 \\
33\text{--}36 & & 37\text{--}8 & & 39\text{--}40 & & 41\text{--}43
\end{array}
$$

Another closing characteristic comes through an association with the original consequent. The repetition in 43–4 gives these last 4 bars a similar structure to 13–16:

Figure 33

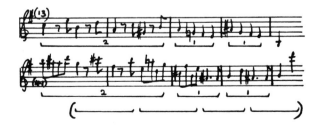

The two 4-bar groups which close the first subject section of the movement return to the regularity of the first theme. Two strongly syncopated bars are offset by two on-beat bars. The 4-bar group is then varied:

Figure 34

The brackets in Figure 34 show the relationship of this 8-bar phrase to Figure 4. References to the thematic features of period 1 are now weak, but they hint at a closing reversal of originally antecedent (x) and consequent (y) material. A familiar figure from the opening sounds at the climactic point ('z'), a fifth above the original (cf. 'a' in Figure 7), signalling the dominant key.

But the strongest 'closing' characteristic is the reduplicative progression of melody and bass-line at the end. The contrapuntal framework moves in parallel octave motion:

Figure 35

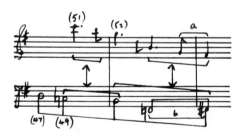

while the very last notes of the cadence mirror the opening counterpoint (cf. 'a' and 'b' above and in Figure 7).

To sum up, the first subject section comprises two periods, of 18 bars and 34 bars. Each begins with the 8-bar first theme, separated from (and linked to) the contrasting consequent by a prolongation. The section is rounded off by an 8-bar phrase which seems to adopt the structure of the first theme, and, to some extent, its material.

Related 8-bar phrases mark off the beginning, middle and end of the section:

$$\underline{8} \; + \; 10 \; + \; \underline{8} \; + \; 18 \; + \; \underline{8}$$

Period 1 is through-composed. Period 2 begins the process of trans-formation, but there are no 'functional' changes the second time round, excepting the temporary antecedent role of the prolongation in 34–7. The arrival of the prolongation in period 2 confirms the principle that period 1 acts as a model, then the first radical transformation takes place. So this is a major turning point in the structure, acting as a pivot for a symmetrical barring of the first subject section:

Period 1			*Period 2*							
8	+	10 │ 8	+	6	+	6	+	6	+	8
8	+	18	+			18			+	8

This ignores the division between periods 1 and 2, but period 1 ends on the dominant, so the first theme in period 2 acts as a small-scale resolution, linking the two:

8	+	10	+	8
I		V		I

The articulation of all these groups shows the influence of the first theme on all other phrases. The first theme divides:

The first prolongation is the only symmetrical 4-bar phrase outside the first theme:

All other 4-bar groups are: 1) articulated like the first theme, in diminution; and 2) linked to a 2-bar group:

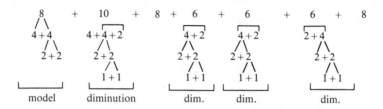

As the first prolongation is therefore distinguished from all consequent phrases, we can count it with the first theme (i), but disassociate the prolongation in period 2 from its 8-bar antecedent (ii). This gives a further arrangement:

$$8 \ + \ 4 \ + \ 6 \ + \ 8 \ + \ 6 \ + \ 6 \ + \ 6 \ + \ 8$$
$$\underset{(i)}{\underbrace{}} \qquad \underset{(ii)}{\underbrace{}}$$
$$18 \quad + \quad 8 \qquad 18 \quad + \quad 8$$

This scheme relies on the strongest points of articulation. We can now superimpose an irregular, a regular and a symmetrical division:

$$8 \ + \ 4 \ + \ 6 \ + \ 8 \ + \ 6 \ + \ 6 \ + \ 6 \ + \ 8$$

1. 8   10   8   18   8
2. 18   8   18   8
3. 8   18   18   8

This structure is typical of Brahms. A similar mixture of conventional and symmetrical structuring appears in the Finale.[3]

The interrupted cadence in the dominant at 44–5 suggests a second subject section. Its first phrase (53–6) remains tonally unstable, but the orchestration and rhythm of this 4-bar phrase show it to be a bridge providing a dramatic contrasting gesture, which enters like a fanfare. For the first time there is a unison entry, and for the first time the strings are silent. There are, however, references to both antecedent and consequent material from the first two periods.

The first four notes of set 1 (Figure 6) are transposed (i), arranged as a descending triad and ascending sixth (ii) with the model anacrusic articulation ('x'):

Figure 36

And the opening changing note motive reappears:

Figure 37

(cf. Figures 7 & 16)

These relationships point to a further treatment of the characteristic material of the opening.

The fanfare acts as a 4-bar incipit in the same way as 1–4 (see Figure 16), but now it is not complemented by a 4-bar consequent. Its function as a contrasting bridge passage separates it from the following 8-bar theme. As the movement expands, the theme is prepared as well as prolonged.

The melody in the dominant beginning at 57 opposes the anacrusic, disjointed, descending character of the first theme. And it is a 2-part invention. Whereas the first theme in period 1 was not counterpointed and in period 2 was combined with various octave reduplications and inversions, the theme now has an apparently strongly contrasting counterpoint. But again it is symptomatic of the dualistic process. While contrasting in texture and character with the first two periods, it grows out of them by making the

thirds background (cf. Figure 6) explicit for the first time. In addition, its
2+2+2+2 articulation recalls the regularity of Figure 4.

However, the varied repetition of 61-2 by 63-4, defined especially by
harmonic repetition, relates the articulation to the prevalent 4+[2+2] pattern mentioned above, particularly since these 8 bars follow on after a diminuted version:

$$2 +[1 + 1] \quad // \quad 4 +[2 + 2]$$

$$\text{diminution} \qquad \text{model form}$$

$$53\text{-}6 \qquad\qquad 57\text{-}64$$

At this stage, then, they are most closely related to the 4-bar group (2+
[1 + 1]): this seems to be confirmed by the relationship of prominent notes
in the 2-part progression, which are either metrically (–) or end (∪) accented
(Figure 38). If they are isolated (i) and subjected to suitable octave transpositions (ii) they give a patterned version of set 1 (cf. Figure 6) of the first
theme (iii, transposed into b minor):

Figure 38

The proportions of the first theme were generated by sequential associations:

$$\begin{array}{ccc} 1 & + & 1 \\ & \searrow \swarrow & \\ 2 & + & 2 \\ & \searrow \swarrow & \\ 4 & + & 4 & = & 8 \end{array}$$

Here the melodic potential of the first 4 bars of period 1 is reproportioned, unfolding at a slower pace:

$$4 \text{ grows to} \qquad 6 \quad + \quad \left[\begin{array}{l} 2 \quad \text{(repeated} \\ \qquad \text{cadence bars)} \end{array} \right]$$

$$8$$

The systematic invention of the opening is being expanded organically: this creates new irregularities, shown, for example, in the harmony of just the first three bars, [1 + 2] (see 'x' in Figure 38). The rigid opening phrase is significantly developed. The articulation follows the 4 + [2 + 2] pattern, but the melody is a development of only the original 4-bar antecedent.

Period 3 shares a common principle of figuration with period 2. In period 2 the figuration is basically a 'doubling', the superimposition of versions of the same material. Figure 39 demonstrates similar octave reduplication in period 3:

Figure 39

The foreground counterpoint (i above) turns out to have a common background with the theme.

The consequent covers bars 65–72. Octave transpositions in the bass transform the counterpoint (Cb., 58 et seq) into a rising figure. It is combined with a version a third higher, in a three-part setting:

Figure 40

The criterion that antecedent and consequent of the first theme have different contrapuntal settings, established in periods 1 and 2, still applies.

By far the most expressive development of the consequent from the antecedent comes in the third bar, where the theme changes from:

Figure 41

i)

to:

ii)

The prominence of this 'A' sets up a strong harmonic development characterized by the chromatic mediant substitution:

Figure 42

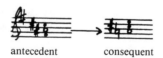

antecedent   consequent

which is revealed in the bass

Figure 43

The 'A' in 67 is the high point of the phrase. It has an interesting long-term preparation (B) and resolution (G) in different registers. 'B' is emphasised in the repeating cadence at the close of the antecedent:

Figure 44

'G' is the harmonic root in the 4 bars (73–6) of the phrase following the theme:

Figure 45

Once again the theme is followed by a prolongation, completing the third step of a large-scale progression which starts on the tonic note:

Figure 46 (cf. Figure 9)

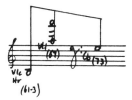

This progression is far less explicit than in period 1. And though it is articulated at regularly spaced points:

$$61 \quad - \quad 67 \quad - \quad 73$$
$$\leftarrow 6 \rightarrow \mid \leftarrow 6 \rightarrow$$

(cf. Figure 9)

the process is expanded.
    The reproportioned theme:

$$\overset{16}{\underset{8 \;+\; 8}{\diagup\diagdown}}$$

influences the prolongation section:

$$\overset{8}{\underset{4 \;+\; 4}{\diagup\diagdown}} \Big\} \text{——— (originally 4)}.$$

Thus the proportions of the opening are retained:

	first theme		prolongation
period 1	8	+	4
period 3	16	+	8

The initial melodic material of the prolongation comes from the 4-bar fanfare (53–6). The cadence uses material from the closing phrase of period 2:

Figure 47

while the bass recalls the preceding first theme consequent:

Figure 48

The first three bars of this phrase follow the 2 + [1 + 1] pattern, with a longer group followed by two shorter ones:

Figure 49

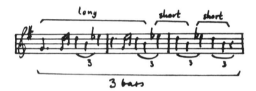

This new proportion – 3 bars – is then exploited in the next phrase. The prolongation is sequenced a fourth higher (from 77): this time, its fourth bar (80) is much more strongly opposed to the first three, through the textural opposition (string pizz., bar 79[4]), and through its clear reference to the rhythm and melodic progression of the original first theme. In these bars associations with different material are more closely juxtaposed than before – the downward semitone relates these different references:

Figure 50

source

bridge

consequent

antecedent

Bar 80 acts as both the eighth bar of the phrase 73–80, and the first bar of a new version of the first theme. This new phrase covers seven bars. The section from the end of the first theme in period 3 to the beginning of the B major section (73 to 86) reveals, therefore, a departure from 8-bar grouping, but the pattern of paired phrases is maintained:

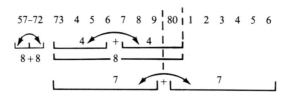

Bar 80 is the first bar to have a double function in the phrasing. This typical device in Brahms's structures is used here as a special effect. The isolated effect of such an ambiguous bar is symptomatic of the unusually rigid phrasing so far.

The 7-bar phrase (80–6) is a solo entry. It is thus associated with the 4-bar fanfare in period 3:

53–6	57–78	80–6
solo	cpt.	solo

It divides into two groups, the length and articulation of the first being the same as at the opening. The string parts imitate the rhythm and some of the shape of the first theme (Figure 51i), and including the wind parts, each 2-bar group falls and rises in the same pattern (Figure 51ii):

Figure 51

i)

ii)

The notes of the first theme are taken at pitch, in the middle of the second subject tonal area. The first four notes (literally, three of the first four) are diminuted:

Figure 52

(1 bar)

(2 bars)

The phrase 81^4–82^3 matches 3–4 in the same way. Taken independently, however, the string notes and the wind notes show a reinforcement of the two kinds of interval of the opening (third and sixth). The third is given twice by the woodwind:

Figure 53

FL

(demonstrating the other first theme features, the direction of the intervals and chromatic relationship). The upward sixth of the first theme is reflected here in the downward string progression:

Figure 54

Altogether, bars 80–3 reproduce most of the notes, and the intervals, of the opening:

Figure 55

The consequent covers three bars. The third descending interval in the consequent of period 1's first theme is now included in the phrase rather than moving into a prolongation ('x' in Figure 56). But the progression of the upper notes resolves according to the norm, on the first note of the next phrase ('y' in Figure 56):

Figure 56

Once again, as in period 3, the consequent of the opening phrase is taken as a model of melodic progression, but this time the pattern of intervals is closely imitated (cf. 'i' in Figure 56).

In period 1 the antecedent is harmonically stable and the consequent becomes unstable through chromatic substitutions. In period 2 these were emphasised in the consequent, with acute false relations (cf. Figure 25). Here they occur in the antecedent (see, for example, Figure 53), the consequent using only notes from the B minor scale. So the order:

stability → tension

has been reversed. This suggests a change of function of the whole phrase. Although it has many features in common with the phrases which opened previous periods, it now acts as a closing phrase to the first section of the second subject.

Explicit melodic, rhythmic and harmonic associations with the opening theme weaken as the exposition progresses. It may be that proportional and articulatory features therefore become stronger associative functions, so that, for instance, this closing phrase is associated not only with the first theme, but also with the closing phrase of the first subject section (45–52). This stresses the influence that the first theme has on phrases with a different formal function and different material.

There has been an expansion in the length of each period:

```
1.  first theme                    prolongation  consequent
         8                    +      | 4      +     6 |          = 18

2.  f. th.        pr. + cons.      pr. + cons.   consequent  closing group
        8      +   |4 + 2|    +    |4 + 2|     +     6    +      8      = 34

3.  fanfare        f.th.           prolongation  closing gr. ( = f.th.)
        4      +   |8 + 8|    +    |4 + 4|    +      7 |               = 35
                                                  'x'
```

The 'prolongation' of period 3 has the most ambiguous character. First, it is based on material from the fanfare: second, it is harmonically equated with the closing group of period 2 — both have 2 × 4 bars in G and C, respectively. In period 2 these harmonies resolve each time within the phrase (see Figure 34). In period 3 they resolve only over the course of the 7-bar final phrase, hence bracket 'x' above. Period 4 continues this growth of longer functional groups:

```
4.    f.th.     prol.  +  cons.          ibid           closing gr.
     |8 + 8|   |4 + 3|  +   4        |5 + 4| + |2 + 8 + 4|     8      = 58
```

In the opening 4 + 4 group (87–94), an explicit first theme reference comes in the consequent, with a row of thirds:

Figure 57

The antecedent uses the downward scale material familiar from period 1's consequent phrase, the closing phrase of period 2 and from the second subject. But the accented notes (* in Figure 58) give a re-ordered version (i) of the familiar opening group (ii):

Figure 58

The 4 bars of the antecedent are articulated by the 2 + [1 + 1] pattern, and in the cadence the accompanying counterpoint gives the changing note motif:

Figure 59

(cf. Figure 7)

The consequent also follows the $2 + [1 + 1]$ pattern:

Figure 60

The bass in the consequent uses an augmented version of an inner part from the antecedent cadence:

Figure 61

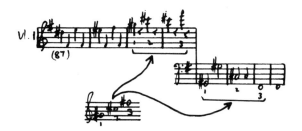

So far, binary associations have belonged to the consequent structure of first themes. In periods 1 and 2, they were melodic relationships:

Figure 62

In period 3 the repeated cadence in bars 5–6 // 7–8 (of the 8-bar group) created a similar articulation. In the 7-bar close of period 3 both harmonic and melodic associations operated in this way (see 'y' in Figure 56). Now a binary association, the augmented progression shown in Figure 61, knits antecedent and consequent together for the first time. This contradicts the acute division at other levels, for the repeated irregularity strongly articulates the 4-bar divisions:

$$\underbrace{2 \; + \; [1 \; + \; 1]} \qquad \underbrace{2 \; + \; [1 \; + \; 1]}$$

The new association across the middle point pulls them together:

Another 8-bar phrase follows, a variation of 87–94. These two phrases therefore stand in the same relationship to each other as the 8 + 8 of period 3. The variation begins with a recasting and inversion of the upper parts, of which the flute and bassoon lines play the simplest version:

Figure 63

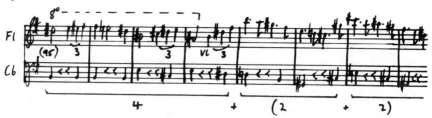

In the consequent of the second phrase, the falling thirds (from Figure 60) are repeated in sequence. The first time they move to V of Fsharp minor (100), a modal transformation of the progression in 91–2, which leads to the dominant major. The sequence then moves to Gsharp minor (102).[4] This 2-bar sequencing restores the 4 + [2 + 2] pattern, and the bass uses the rhythm of the first theme:

Figure 64

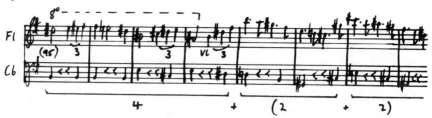

The accompaniment provides, for the first time, a marked rhythmic distinction between antecedent

This second pattern links together consequent and prolongation in contrast to the gradual dislocation of the two in periods 1 and 2. They mould together melodically in the manner of period 1, and the effect is strengthened here by a new rising line in the consequent:

Figure 65

The bass-line confirms this fusion of first theme and prolongation:

Figure 66

These four bars, then, no longer follow the pattern of acting as a distinct group. In one respect they are related to the most disassociated earlier prolongation group, for the overall rhythm of the top line ('x' in Figure 65) is that of the prolongation which first acted as an antecedent (34–7; cf. Figure 30'x'). But they are generally more integrated with the first theme phrases than before.

The following 4-bar group (107–10) to some extent takes on the role of prolongation. It is the most gesturally isolated passage so far, an extended diminished chord with the first entry of the timpani with an 'atmospheric' pianissimo roll. But it follows the tendency of previous prolongations, for it is static: only the subdued string figures and trumpet rhythm give the group any contour.

The 4-bar consequent (110–13) uses material from the fanfare of period 3 (which was subsequently absorbed into a prolongation). There is the same kind of irregular phrasing as in period 3, with an ambiguous bar (110) which elides two groups:

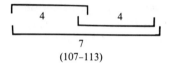

(107–113)

The 2 + [1 + 1] pattern is reversed:

Figure 67

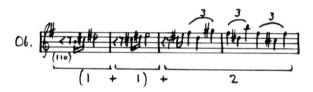

as is the position of first theme material, for the opening changing-note motif is now a background to the prolongation and consequent sections (103–113):

Figure 68

(cf. Fig. 7)

The prolongation / consequent group is extended:

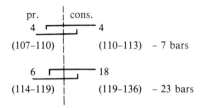

The varied prolongation (114–119) completes a long movement of the bass down to the dominant:

Figure 69

a 'closing' progression, by association with the closing phrase of period 2 (see Figure 35). Period 2 is also recalled by a 2-bar extension of the prolongation:

Figure 70

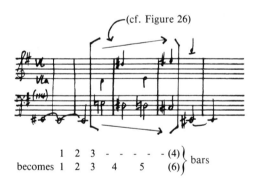

And the 4 + 2 articulation of the following 6-bar group (119–125) recalls the 6-bar groups towards the end of period 2.

Symphony No. 4 in E Minor

In the long consequent extension (119–136), the substitution of a D major version of the fanfare gives a rising thirds background (i):

Figure 71

which refers to set 2 of the opening background (cf. (ii) above, the first theme consequent transposed to B). This is one of the few explicit references to set 2, and it comes near the close of the exposition.

The final cadences cover eight bars, leading to a repeated imperfect cadence. Brahms attempts to mask the squareness by extending 2 beats of the dominant into the tonic group:

Figure 72

The closing phrase is a regular $4 + 4$ (136^4–144), which closely imitates the texture and rhythm of the first theme.

The exposition shows unconventional material used in a symphonic structure. Even without the suggestion from the Finale we can identify a Chaconne element. It is normal for the material of sections with different functions (first subject, transition, second subject, closing phrases) to be integrated. Less conventional, however, is the recurring sequence of phrases (first theme, prolongation, consequent), with the proportions of first theme to prolongation unchanged. The exposition, therefore, shows a mixed form, reconciling the idea of transformed repetition — that is, a variation process — with the sonata process. Our analysis has attempted to show how the repetitions are transformed to accommodate the functions of a sonata form.

This view of the tense process in the exposition accounts for the lack of conventional motivic work. The second subject, for instance, is, for Brahms, rather crudely invented. Perhaps because he is so involved in Chaconne-type reproduction, he falls into a kind of repetitiveness on one level (the rhythm) which he normally took pains to avoid:

Vlc., 57–64: ♩ ♩ | ♩ ♩ ♩ ♩   ×4

The transformations which move forward the sonata structure are often far more subtle than the repetitive characteristics: the tension between the two processes of the mixed form — Chaconne and sonata — often swings in favour of the Chaconne, because the repetitive characteristics are so strong.

Contributing to this, and complementing the lack of motivic work, is the prevalent octave reduplication, which is implicit in the opening theme, and therefore frequent in the exposition. The contrapuntal drive which results from a superimposition of independent melodic structures (e.g., in the prolongation) is reserved for consequent phrases. Those phrases on which the weight of the sonata form falls — the openings of the four periods — are figured by octave reduplications and simple inversions, despite their complex texture.

There is little tension in the form of contrast in the main material, and such as it is, it cannot be exploited while it is confined by the Chaconne principle. The real contrasting gesture comes with the fanfare group, and although it is derived from the main material, it is never taken into the first theme transformations. In its introductory position, and then by its fusion with the prolongation phrases, it is brought into close juxtaposition with the first theme. But this serves to stress the division between this theme (the Chaconne element) and the sonata process. It is also symptomatic that the exposition is, for Brahms, harmonically limited. His normal sturdy functional and sequential progressions are not punctuated by typical substitutions which demand long-term resolution.

This harmonic character of the exposition predicts some rearrangement of the phrase sequence (or a weakening of Chaconne relationships) in the development section, for a traditional development must introduce a more radical tonal process.

In the development, the elements of the exposition are distilled into two groups — first theme and prolongation/fanfare. They appear in the expected sequence, as seen in the chart on the following page.

Symphony No. 4 in E Minor

Divisions of 148–227

```
                  148    153    157    165    169    173
                   T      P      T      P      Ta    Ta→
                   8  +   4      8  +   4      4  +  4 +7

                      ┌──── e ────┐  ┌── g ──┐  ┌ bflat ────────────────┐
              period:      5           6                         7
                        └────────────────┬────────────────────────────┘
                                         39


    184      188      192      196      202      206      210      214
    P/F       P        P        P       P/F       F        F       Fc
     4    +   4    +   4    +  4+2   +   4    +    4    +   4    +   5
         └────────────────────────────┬────────────────────────────┘
                                       35


                  219    227
                   T      P
                   8  +   20
                      ┌ gsharp ┐
              period:      8
                        └──┬──┘
                           28
```

KEY:

    T = first theme or transformation
  Ta = first theme antecedent transformation
    P = prolongation
    F = fanfare
  P/F = prolongation and fanfare combined
  Fc = fanfare triplets set in consequent-type scale
  → = phrase extension

The only tonally stable sections are the first theme transformations (see under 'T' and 'Ta' in the chart on p. 78). The unstable sections ('P' and 'F' in the chart) use sequence, chromatic bass-lines joining up distant harmonies (often like sequences) and functional relationships characterized by interrupted cadences (183–4, 209–10) and unconfirmed dominant progressions (V–I(= V), e.g., 210–19).

The four periods each begin with a first theme phrase, and their sequence follows to some extent that of periods 1–4:

Periods

1 and 5: 8-bar first theme, similar prolongations

2 and 6: octave reduplication, quaver figuration

3 and 7: 2-part contrapuntal setting, double phrase (8 + 8 in period 3, 4 + 4 in period 7)

4 and 8: legato wind and pizz. strings in antecedent, ♩♩♩ rhythm.
       3

Period 5, which matches period 1, suggests that the exposition will be repeated (especially if we assume the expectation of a literal exposition repeat, as in a classical symphony). So the new tonal shift (to G minor) after period 5 has great force. Here the expectations of the Chaconne procedure contribute to the sonata process: their contradiction by a new key (see 153–7) reinforces the impact of the tonal development.

The third period in both exposition and development begins with a double transformation. In the exposition, period 3, beginning with an 8-bar phrase articulated as in period 1, stretches the material of the first theme over 16 bars (8 + 8). In the traditionally exciting position of a development section (the first climax) Brahms now uses a 4 + 4 group rather than 8 + 8. In the terms of material this is not a contraction, for each 4-bar group uses the 4-bar material of the opening. But in relation to period 3, period 7 adopts the proportions of a different process, the fragmentation of a development section rather than the broadening of a second subject.

Both period 3 and period 7 end with an irregular phrase of 7 bars, created in period 3 by elision and in period 7 by phrase extension (177–8), sequence (179–80) and an extended cadence (181–3).

The development section is about 2/3 the length of the exposition — 102 bars compared to 144. The proportion of first theme groups to other groups is, however, the same if we add up the number of bars in each division:

	first theme	*prol., cons., fanfare etc.*
exposition	55 bars	89
development	39	63

(If the development section ratio 39:63 is expressed as a function of approximately 144, i.e., the number of bars in the exposition, it turns out to be 55:89.) But the 35-bar prolongation/fanfare section in period 7 gives consequent material a more significant role in the process of development than it had in the exposition. This regrouping of material enabled Brahms to develop a long section of roving tonality (period 7). An intervening first theme phrase, which is by definition tonally stable, would have either halted this momentum or would have had to lose its tonal stability.

In line with a normal development section, motives are transformed more explicitly than in the exposition. Two examples show this craftsmanship. The first is 'variational', showing various characterized versions of the opening third:

Figure 73

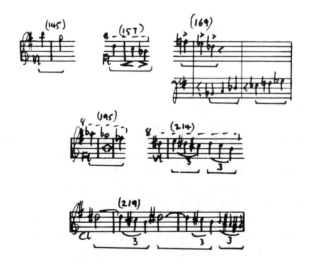

A second example shows more functional workings, where the opening counterpoint is used in antecedent figuration as an explicit motive rather than a melodic background:

Figure 74

(cf. Figure 7)

Even a cursory examination of the development has shown that it continues the mixed form of the exposition. Consequent material takes the weight of development. It is hard to see how Brahms could have brought his Chaconne element very far into the process: when he tries to do so, the difficulties are clear. The reduplications of his most 'developed' transformation (the first theme in period 7, 169 et seq) seem pedantic, particularly as canonic (x) and inversional settings (y) have been heard before (cf. periods 1 and 3):

Figure 75

Period 8 has a melodic variation (cf. C1. and string parts) of the type which Brahms himself considered to be merely decorative (cf. Chapter 2). Only the new tonality of these transformations adds significantly to the exposition, and it seems to be consequent material which really gets the tonal process off the ground.

The conflict between the repetitive and the dynamic is most acute at the end of the development. Following the orthodox, 35-bar crescendo of period 7, period 8 has an 8-bar first theme transformation and a 20-bar prolongation. The principle of static prolongation is carried to its extreme, for each of these 20 bars repeats the rhythm:

The melodic figures and harmony articulate the group thus:

This prepares for the recapitulation at the expense of a kind of abrupt change in pace (cf. period 7/period 8) which conflicts with the idea of a smoothly organized symphonic development.

The recapitulation begins with an augmentation to 12 bars (246^3–258) of the 4-bar first theme antecedent, followed by its 4-bar consequent. This is the first time that the proportions of the first theme have changed at the beginning of a period: it complements the broadening at the end of the development. The first three notes of the opening are lengthened (246^3–248) and the fourth is prolonged over 4 bars (249–52), with the string figuration and timpani roll which have become archetypal for prolongations, in the development: the six bars are then sequenced. At the end of the second group an F natural sounds briefly; this together with the notes B and G in the held parts gives a V^7 chord in C, resolving onto C at the beginning of the consequent. This harmonic link is a new feature in the first theme.[5] The differentiation between a radically transformed antecedent and a normal consequent (259–62) brings to the foreground the subtle contrast within the first theme (see Figure 16).

This passage demonstrates the possibility mentioned above of taking consequent material into the model. The fact that Brahms does so at this point indicates his desire elsewhere to set up a mixed form, with an independent element subjected to Chaconne-type transformations rather than symphonic development, for this is the only such restructuring in the movement. It is possible, but unique.

The recapitulation abbreviates the transitional period (period 2 in the exposition), and here the tonal change is made to bring period 3 back in the tonic (cf. 27–44 and 281–8). Brahms follows his normal procedure of using a 'second development' (369–413), before bringing back the closing phrase from period 2 (414–421) and ending with a 19-bar coda.

The climax of the second development is a heroic version of the first theme (393⁴–401). Here, the prevalent octave reduplications surface as canon, with a new regular rhythm in the consequent driving home the original background of thirds:

Figure 76

Evans[6] took note of this climactic phrase, in an article which suggested some sort of passacaglia-based interpretation of the movement:

> (The first movement) not only subjects its themes and motives to passacaglia treatment within the symphonic 'cadre', but it seems during its coda actually to prophesy, as it were, the ultimate triumph of its passacaglia element. No great effort of imagination is required to place this interpretation upon the pompous delivery of the original theme, which commences at bar 394. . . .

5

Brahms the Progressive and
Intermezzo, Op. 119, No. 1

INTRODUCTION

To avoid confusion between the review of *Brahms the Progressive* and the illustrative analysis of the *Intermezzo, Op. 119 No. 1,* the analysis is set off from the text by horizontal lines.

BRAHMS THE PROGRESSIVE

The quality of *Style and Idea* is caught by a reviewer of the first version,[1] who speaks of *'aperçus'* of the highest order.[2] The same evocative description is echoed in Goehr's review[3] of the second version.[4] In the essay *Brahms the Progressive* the insights are often more compelling than the arguments.

To the extent that Schoenberg does pursue a thesis, he has gained little sympathy. Dean, for example, was less impressed by the *'aperçus'* than by what seemed to him a flawed chain of thought. His cavil rests on a question of historical perspective:

> Wagner is allowed to have 'contributed to the development of structural formulations through his technique of repetitions, varied or unvaried' – surely a classical instance of damnation with faint praise – but Schubert is not discussed, and the Russian nationalists are not even mentioned.[5]

In view of this, he finds Schoenberg's conclusion that Brahms inaugurated the progress towards an unrestricted musical language 'startling'. This is typical of the way Schoenberg was misunderstood: he was not concerned with a thorough historical essay.

In criticising Schoenberg's emphasis in his view of the nineteenth century, Dean misses the important stage of the argument — that Brahms at least contributed to the progress. This idea was not a common one at the time, and it attracted interest only slowly. Rubsamen's *Schoenberg in America*[6] refers frequently to *Style and Idea* without mentioning the Brahms essay. It is even more surprising that Gal, with a decade of hindsight on *Brahms the Progressive,* fails to mention Schoenberg in his concluding chapter, 'Contemporary World and Posterity'.[7] The publication of a fuller *Style and Idea* will probably attract more attention to the essay: Goehr's review calls it 'superlative'. And a recent Brahms study makes the explicit connection between Brahms's and Schoenberg's music, in an examination of the late works.[8]

The directness of Schoenberg's title is not reflected in the style and organization of the essay. The connection of ideas is often obscure, and there are many distracting asides. But these usually underline Schoenberg's intention of expressing not only a comparative notion of 'progressive', but also his belief that the progress was valuable.

He prepares for this judgment in sections I and II. First, two traditional neuroses of the Brahms literature are discussed. Schoenberg regards the unattractive side of Brahms's character as the composer's natural defence: his own experiences of Viennese hostility put him in sympathy with Brahms's bitterness. He also deals with the Wagner/Brahms controversy, characterizing it with a point which is rarely remembered:

> ...those who disliked Wagner clung to Brahms, and vice versa. There were many who disliked both. They were, perhaps, the only non-partisans. (p. 399)

In section II Schoenberg discusses musical 'comprehensibility'. To prepare for an account of Brahms's rich harmonic style, complex proportional relationships and sophisticated motivic organization, he suggests that a development away from the simplest musical relationships is appropriate for a certain kind of listener:

> Repeatedly hearing things which one likes is pleasant and need not be ridiculed. There is a subconscious desire to understand better and realize more details of the beauty. But an alert and well-trained mind will demand to be told the more remote matters, the more remote consequences of the simple matters that he has already comprehended. (p. 401)

Schoenberg does not elaborate on this, perhaps because he is not putting forward an argument so much as stating a belief — that the development of more complex music is a natural process, and is worthwhile *per se.* Music, he claims, has both aesthetic pleasure and beauty, just as language has rhyme, rhythm, metre and so on, as well as feelings and thoughts (p. 399). But with his first musical example, Schoenberg seems to change this position:

> Evenness, regularity, symmetry, subdivision, repetition, unity, relationship in rhythm and harmony and even logic — none of these elements produces or even contributes to beauty. . . . one finds numerous slightly varied repetitions, as in the otherwise very beautiful *Blue Danube Waltz*. (p. 399 and Example 1)

The formal elements Schoenberg cites cannot contribute to beauty, yet he implies that they can detract from it: what spoils the 'otherwise very beautiful' waltz is a formal element, the recurring varied repetition. The same conflict arises later, when Schoenberg follows an account (p. 435) of the articulation of Example 46 with: 'In Brahms' notation these subcutaneous beauties are accommodated. . .' Again, formal finesse is described in terms of beauty.

These difficulties hinge on Schoenberg's two oppositions: between beauty and aesthetic effect, and between simple and complex aesthetic effect. The first of these might be better expressed as a distinction between musical ideas and musical continuity. The main point of the argument is that complex continuity (as in Brahms) is a progress over simple continuity (of the Hollywood 'lyric' type, see p. 400). Less clear, however, is Schoenberg's view about the first opposition — witness the several ways he describes the genesis of 'aesthetic value': form (p. 399), exploitation of the potency of. . . components (ibid.), organization (ibid.), methods of presentation (p. 401). This, together with the slight inconsistencies noted above, suggests that he is not as convinced of an opposition between beauty (or ideas) and aesthetic effect (or continuity) as he first implies. It might be conjectured that, despite a wish to rationalize his sensitivity to musical organization, especially after a lifetime of criticism, Schoenberg could not avoid associating sophisticated construction with his own concept of beauty.

The discussion of comprehensibility and the attraction of complex music leads to a straightforward summary and programme, which opens section III:

> Progress in music consists in the development of methods of presentation which correspond to the conditions just discussed. It is the purpose of this essay to prove that Brahms, the classicist, the academician, was a great innovator in the realm of musical language, that, in fact, he was a great progressive. (p. 401)

With this, it finally becomes clear that Schoenberg is not answering the typical criticisms of Brahms: he is exposing his role in a historical progression, which Schoenberg felt himself to represent, but in which Brahms had hardly been recognized.

The typical criticisms were of Brahms's 'ideas'. Gal, for example, quotes Weingartner's report of a critic's view, that '(Brahms) works exceedingly well with ideas which he does not have.'[9] And Weingartner's own unease is quoted:

> ...I was able to admire its (referring to Brahms's music) workmanship and construction and to derive the same type of enjoyment from it that a physician may experience in laying bare the musculature of a well-grown corpse. If, however, I tried to submit to a spontaneous impression, I would experience that paralyzing disillusion which would befall the physician who had the temerity to try to bring the corpse back to life.[10]

Schoenberg would consider such views to be of no interest; but at least he could hope for a new appreciation of Brahms in the realm of musical language. He is concerned with the recognition of aesthetic value rather than a defence of Brahms's inspiration.[11]

The first recognition he seeks is for Brahms's harmonic innovation (section IV), his example being the opening of the *String Quartet in C minor, Op. 51 No. 1*. He regards the first theme itself as 'daring' for the ears of the time in its harmonic richness. But the middle section (given in Example 3) is compared with Wagner and 'even the most progressive composers after Brahms'. Once again, Schoenberg goes on to lose some clarity in the argument of these examples. He adds two earlier cases of a similar procedure, from Beethoven and Schubert, without making it clear whether this makes Brahms less progressive (as it would seem to). Schoenberg is so concerned with the tradition of musical language (and so honest, where he could have made a point by omission) that he must show its genesis, even at the expense of his argument.

The harmony of *Op. 119i* is even more radical than Schoenberg's example, though in a different way. It does have some strong chromaticism in substitute harmonies (which Schoenberg finds characteristic of Wagner and to his credit, p. 405), for example in 13–5. And chromatically related triads (in inverted chords, mentioned in Schoenberg under Example 8) colour the consequent of the first phrase in the middle section (21–4, triads on D–Dsharp–E–Esharp–Fsharp–G). The greatest innovation of the piece, however, is of a kind which Schoenberg mentions only in passing, asking Wagner's harmony to be compared with: '...the Rhapsody, Op. 79 No. 2, which almost avoids establishing a tonality' (p. 405).[12]

Op. 119i avoids establishing a tonality at the opening through the obscurity of its harmonic formation. The opening melodic idea and its varied repetition:

Figure 1

are accompanied for 3 bars by groups of descending thirds. The thirds tend to form triadic relationships; however, these bars are equally suggestive of a contrapuntal invention, where the horizontal structure of each part is more comprehensible than the background succession of vertical relationships. Although the descent stops on the third beat in 1, suggesting the harmonic relationship of a falling fifth:

Figure 2

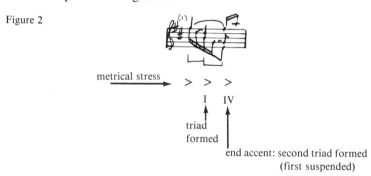

the second bar makes this weak harmonic articulation ambiguous, by continuing the descending thirds onto the final semiquaver. The effect of a sequence:

$$1 \quad / \quad 2$$
$$I \, - \, IV \quad VII \, - \, III$$

is brought about both by the end-accent now on the final semiquaver (D) and the formation of major and minor thirds in the first two beats, which creates a minor (dominant) seventh chord, with its root on A (the fourth semiquaver). Thus the sense of harmonic definition through alternate stress of the metre in the first bar (which is mainly a learned response, as the metre is hardly defined until the first bar is over) is contradicted in the second:

Figure 3

Triadic relationships, weakened by these ambiguities, are also chal-
lenged by the overall relationship of an ascending sequence between 1 and 2,
which relates the root notes of 1 to the wrong notes in the next bar:

Figure 4

The third bar goes on to repeat the pattern of Figure 3, beginning on
Csharp, so that the sequential relationship (Figure 4) is established no more
firmly than the triadic progression. The implied sequence of triads continues into 4, where harmonic relationships are clarified in the more homophonic texture:

Figure 5

But this sequence of chords is neither aurally explicit nor analytically
demonstrable in a systematic way.

Where there are only implicit harmonic relationships, that is, where
the vertical succession is not made comprehensible by the rhythm and tex-

ture, repetition is an important structuring force. Here the repetitions emphasize groupings which duplicate, in part, the harmonic progression shown in Figure 5. But whereas Figure 5 shows a harmonic background which is articulated within the metre, Figure 6 shows a symmetrical relationship, which crosses the bar-lines in a hemiola pattern. In addition, while reinforcing the harmonic bass-line, it contradicts the idea of triadic grouping:

Figure 6

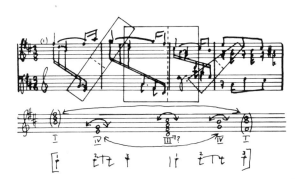

This acute harmonic ambiguity prohibits the definition of a key. Its complexity, however, has little to do with Schoenberg's cases of remote harmony pulling away from a tonal centre. The opening 3 bars in fact fulfil one condition of tonal definition — the exclusive use of all the notes of a key. Not only are the notes of D major used exclusively, but each note is repeated at least once:

Figure 7

However, these notes also make up the (descending melodic) minor scale of B: the first three notes of the piece form the tonic triad of B minor (which also closes the symmetrical organization of Figure 6); and the two suspensions of the (antecedent) melody resolve on its dominant and tonic notes

(Figure 8i), while the melodic background begins a progression which drives towards the tonic (Figure 8ii):

Figure 8

Brahms chooses to resolve the tonal ambiguity in B minor, altering the A's of Figure 7 to Asharp, in 4. But a resolution which could be substituted for 4–5 follows immediately:

Figure 9

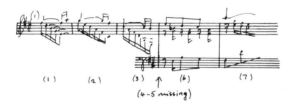

This substitutive relationship, with a sequence in the consequent:

1 2 3 4 5 6 7 8

realizing the latent progression of the antecedent:

1 2 3 4 5 6 7 8

produces a radical kind of ambiguity in relation to the conventional articulation. As Schoenberg says in a later example of an 8-bar phrase:

> ...if eight measures constitute an aesthetic principle, it is preserved here in spite of the great freedom of construction. (p. 436)

In choosing harmonic richness as a test of 'progress', Schoenberg has noted a quality which is typical of Brahms. But there are other kinds of progress related to Schoenberg's concerns. The questions raised by the opening of *Op. 119i* are how it defines a tonality and how it moves from a quasi-harmonic idea (the first bar of descending thirds) to quasi-harmonic continuity (until the explicit harmony of the fourth bar). The first is the kind of question Schoenberg tackled in the *Harmonielehre*,[13] as Goehr explains:

> ...the principles of chord substitutions and the way of altering them so as to overlap new scales and non-tonal vertical constellations, are described in the *Harmonielehre*, and nowhere else.[14]

But Goehr goes on to summarize what Schoenberg failed to do:

> Schoenberg never found the theoretical system of relating continuity and idea in the same way. Had he done so he would have left us a theoretical diary of the functioning of the twelve-note technique in relation to the harmonic and polyphonic practices of his own tonal music, early or late.[15]

Specifically, in this context, he would have been able to connect the complex harmonic ambiguity of the few examples in Brahms like *Op. 119i* with his own language, instead of relying in the essay on the more commonplace practice of harmonic richness.

In section V Schoenberg again compares Brahms with Wagner. He notes that Wagner's *Leitmotiven* not only generate the modulatory character shared by dramatic music and 'rounded form' such as the symphony or sonata, but also 'fulfil...an organizational task'. The point is that:

> ...if foresight in organization is called formalistic in the case of Brahms, then this organization is also formalistic, because it stems from the same state of mind, from one which conceives an entire work in a single creative moment and acts accordingly. (p. 405)

Schoenberg's example of 'foresight in the case of Brahms' from the *Fourth Symphony* has found its way into much of the subsequent literature and many books on analysis. It may be that it has caught the imagination of musicians in reaction to the common practice of showing motivic correspondences, which do not necessarily suggest 'spontaneity'. Schoenberg wishes to distinguish between this and construction, to reply to Brahms criticism, without moving on to questions of 'beauty':

> It would look like a high accomplishment of intellectual gymnastics if all this had been 'constructed' prior to inspired composing. (p. 407)

Despite his bland presentation, it seems from the emphasis of Schoenberg's analysis that the greatest art of the example is not the simple relationship between the theme of the first movement and the variation pattern (Example 12), but the combinative association of the main themes of the first and final movements (Example 12 and Example 13). The descending thirds reveal a common background.[16]

The first phrase of *Op. 119i* shows similar workings: they seem to be equally 'inspirational', the quality which Schoenberg is at such pains to express:

> People generally do not know that luck is a heavenly gift...Sceptics might attempt belittling this as a mere 'lucky chance'. Such people have a wrong evaluation of both luck and inspiration and are not capable of imagining what both can achieve. (p. 406)

It is shown above that the antecedent defines a tonality in the exclusive use of all the notes of a key, and that the ambiguity of the scale used (which defines D major and B [melodic] minor) is resolved in the minor in 4. There are symmetrically or harmonically determined repetitions of all the notes (see Figures 6 and 7), but the succession of thirds establishes a separate organizing principle which demands to be continued. A complete cycle of thirds using only one scale will repeat itself on the seventh step, and will have presented the notes of the complete scale. It does so without repeating any note of the scale, so that if there are intervening repetitions, they create harmonic attractions: this function of repetition was, of course, a basic consideration in the evolution of a twelve-tone system. The antecedent exposes two cycles of thirds:

Figure 10

As the cycle begins on Fsharp, the final note is decisive in the ambiguity between D major and B minor: here the first cycle ends on A (D) and the second on Asharp (B).

The same pair of third cycles is a background to the 4 consequent bars. The explicit progression by thirds is replaced by homophonic presentation, which partly articulates the implied harmony of the antecedent (see Figure 5):

Figure 11

*substituted for IV (cf. Figure 5)

The irregular articulation in the foreground relationships (see above) has, therefore, a regular repeating background:

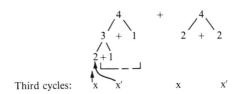

This shows only one of many combinative relationships in *Op. 119i*. Its sophistication can be judged by the fact that in 4–7 the melody and bass are canonically related, so that the notes of the bass-line are each multifunctional, related canonically to certain melody notes, harmonically to different notes through the association of the thirds cycle, and melodically to the overall progression of the antecedent melody, in an inversional relationship:

Figure 12

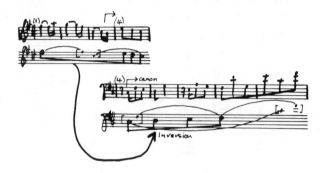

It is even less likely than in Schoenberg's example that these bars could have been 'constructed prior to inspired composing'. There are no generally known rules for constructing such complex relationships.

In section VI Schoenberg once more starts a line of thought from abstract discussion to examples in Brahms (which arrive in section X). This part of the essay again begins with the question of the relationship between 'idea' and 'function'. But now the emphasis is changed: 'I wish to join ideas with ideas' (p. 407). It is not made clear whether he means in his own music or in Brahms's. And there is no need, for the conclusion expresses, with some force, that Schoenberg believes this to be the important issue in composition:

> ...no space should be devoted to mere formal purposes...those segments or sections which fulfil structural requirements should do so without being mere trash. (p. 408)

The thoughts connecting these statements dwell mainly on the notion that function serves idea, and not vice versa. But one passage goes beyond this:

> No matter what the purpose or meaning of an idea in aggregate may be...it must be an idea which had to take this place even if it were not to serve for this purpose or meaning or function. (p. 407)

The implication of 'had to take this place' is that there is a logic which governs the succession of ideas, a continuity independent of the functions of musical language. Schoenberg never found a full theory to account for this logic, which explains the brief, implicit reference here. The functions of musical language, however, were thoroughly investigated. This distinction is equally clear in *Fundamentals of Musical Composition:*

> Artistically, the connexion of motive-forms depends on factors which can only be discussed at a later stage. However, the mechanics of combination can be described and demonstrated, while temporarily disregarding the stiffness of some of the resulting phrases. [17]

This may explain an obscure sequence of thought which leads into the second part of section VI. Schoenberg notes that he is speaking personally:

> This is no critique of classic music — it merely presents my personal artistic code of honour which everybody else may disregard. (p. 408)

Nevertheless, he uses the 'code of honour' to qualify the next statement:

> But it seems to me that the progress in which Brahms was operative should have stimulated composers to write music for adults. (ibid.)

The understatement here rests in the 'but'. It could be interpreted as meaning: given that the highest value of a composition is the quality and continuity of its ideas, why should Brahms, at the same time as pursuing this aesthetic shared by all composers, not participate in a development of the musical language?

As this is the crux of Schoenberg's argument (though he does not say so), it is worth illustrating from his own analogy:

> Why should it not be possible in music to say in whole complexes in a condensed form what, in the preceding epochs, had at first to be said several times with slight variations before it could be elaborated? Is it not as if a writer who wanted to tell of 'somebody who lives in a house near the river' should have to explain what a house is, what it is made for, and of what material, and, after that, explain the river in the same way? (ibid.)

Schoenberg is talking about musical language, or function or construction. But he might have indicated what ideas are and how they are connected, at least in the verbal analogy. It is not for the musician to explain why the ideas 'somebody', 'a house' and 'the river' are related. But the conjunction of these ideas clearly has its logic, or its continuity, independent of the functional, or grammatical relationship: this is evident by comparison, for instance, with the three ideas – 'somebody' 'antimatter' and '2/3', or with 'somebody who grows a house inside the river'.

Schoenberg goes on to show the historical tradition of the kind of progress he is examining. He rejects the aesthetic of the early classical style (section VII), assuming that it was an imposed aesthetic which ignored the internal logic of music, and concentrates on construction in Haydn and Mozart (section VIII). In passing, he suggests why there is an apparent contradiction in the progress of classical music through Beethoven:

> One might...wonder why in Haydn's and Mozart's forms irregularity is more frequently present than in Beethoven's. Is it perhaps that formal finesses have diverted a listener's attention, which should concentrate upon the tremendous power of emotional expression? (p. 409)

The irregularities of Mozart's music are for Schoenberg a result of dramatic necessity. He believes that Mozart anticipates the dramatic demands of a 'finale', 'ensemble' or even 'aria' by beginning with varied material:

> ...phrases of various lengths and characters, each of them pertaining to a different phase of the action and the mood. They are, in their first formulation, loosely joined together, and often simply[18] juxtaposed, thus admitting to be broken asunder and used independently as motival material for small formal segments. (p. 411)

Having stressed his personal debt to Mozart (at the beginning of section IX), Schoenberg returns to the relationship between Brahms and Wagner. Wagner shows that irregularity and asymmetry are not inevitable in dramatic construction, as he 'seldom abandoned a two-by-two-measure construction' (p. 414); however, both composers strove for progress in 'musical prose'.

The concept of musical prose is defined in several stages. First, it is distinguished from:

> ...a baroque sense of form, that is,...a desire to combine unequal, if not heterogeneous, elements into a formal unit. (p. 411)

Later, a Mozart example (Example 21) shows with great enthusiasm what Schoenberg considers it to be:

> ...(the quality of being) prose-like in the unexcelled freedom of its rhythm and the perfect independence from formal symmetry. (p. 416)

In section X the historical perspective is added; talking of examples from Brahms, Schoenberg notes:

> Though these irregularities do not measure up to the artfulness of the Mozart examples, they still present a more advanced phase of the development toward liberation from formal restrictions of musical thoughts, because they do not derive from a baroque feeling, or from the necessities of illustration, as is the case in dramatic music. (p. 417–8)

It is typical of Schoenberg's conviction and the thoroughness, however obscure, of the essay, that even before he has defined this type of construction (p. 416, see above), he lays down its artistic implications:

> (...the alert mind of an educated listener)...enables a musician to write for upper-class minds, not only doing what grammar and idiom require, but, in other respects lending to every sentence the full pregnancy of meaning of a maxim, of a proverb, or an aphorism. This is what musical prose should be – a direct and straightforward presentation of ideas, without any patchwork, without mere padding and empty repetitions.[19]
> (p. 415)

This refers to the first opposition mentioned above. 'In other respects' means in the logic of continuity of musical ideas, to which the aesthetic effect of musical prose cannot contribute, in principle (p. 399). And the quotation also echoes section VI – '...no space should be devoted to mere formal purposes'.

Schoenberg's demonstration of musical prose in Brahms (section X) uses examples mainly from the songs – presumably a tactical decision in view of the many instrumental examples he could have chosen. He shows 'prose-like' construction, not in opposition to cases of dramatic necessity, but in contexts where it supplements the poetic demands (see Examples 27–35, and commentary).

The instrumental examples (Examples 22–4) reveal irregular phrasing, a feature which 'already appear(s) in the earliest works...' (p. 416).[20] This is the least informative part of the essay. In analysing the opening of the *Sextet in B flat, Op. 18,* for example, Schoenberg invites a comparison with the second sextet, *Op. 36.* The opening of *Op. 18* is regarded as part of the development of musical prose, with its 10-bar phrase divided as $3 + 2 + 2 + 1$.[21] If this has the significance Schoenberg claims, it suggests that there must be a significant explanation for Brahms's return, in the next sextet, to regular construction. The exposition of *Op. 36* proceeds mostly by regularly articulated 8-bar phrases: such irregularities as there are concern the occasional 2- or 4-bar extension. In general, Brahms is as happy with what Schoenberg tentatively calls the 'aesthetic principle' of the 8-bar phrase (p. 436)[22] as he is with musical prose.[23]

Again, Schoenberg only hints at an important development in Brahms. He says of Example 24 (from the Scherzo of *Op. 36*):

> ...the most interesting feature is presented by the ambiguity of the ending of the second phrase. One wonders whether measures 9ff. do not belong to this phrase. (p. 417)

Yet his analytical markings on Example 24 do not seem to capture the ambiguity. Uncharacteristically, he ignores the harmonic shaping, which places the second phrase (which might be called a consequent) in a weak relationship to the cadential background:

```
    1       2       3       4       5      6    7    8      9    10    11
g:I(-IV)  I(-IV)  I(-V)   I(-V)   IV-VII                   II   V    II   V....
                                  Bflat:V   I   IV         I   VII

_____   _ _         _ _ _____
g:            I                                  V
```

Similarly, the beginning of the third phrase (9ff. in Schoenberg's analysis) is strongly related to the second (5–8): as Schoenberg implies, it is an extension rather than the beginning of a new 8-bar period, but this becomes clearer when the analysis focuses on repetitive elements:

Figure 13

In comparison with many themes in Brahms, however, these examples show little ambiguity in any case. The most typical ambiguities are not of the successive variety shown by Schoenberg, but of simultaneous types of organization. Rather than relying on ambiguity of phrase and proportion, they are contrapuntally ambiguous, with different levels of organization in vertical conflict (see, for example, the opening bars of *Op. 119i* in the above analysis). This produces tense internal articulation (of the type examined in Chapter 2), but the principle of regular phrasing is often maintained.

However this may be, Schoenberg's interest is not in the simple fact of musical prose, but in the organizing potential of prose-like relationships, which are implicit in the first presentation of an idea:

> The most important capacity of a composer is to cast a glance into the most remote future of his themes or motives. He has to be able to know beforehand the consequences which derive from the problems existing in his material, and to organize everything accordingly. Whether he does this consciously or subconsciously is a subordinate matter. It suffices if the result proves it. (p. 422)

Section XI reveals this foresight in Beethoven's *String Quartet in F minor, Op. 95,* where Schoenberg illustrates relationships of pitch.

Op. 119i can be examined in the light of these ideas to reveal modelling of a different type: a few examples will be chosen.

The first concerns overall structuring. The piece falls almost unambiguously into the following divisions:

$$8 \; + \; 8 \;\; / \;\; 14 \; + \; *12 \; + \; 4 \;\; / \;\; 8 \; + \; 13$$
$$\underline{\text{A}} \qquad \underline{\text{B}} \qquad \underline{\text{A}}$$

keys: b D b

The two prominent recapitulations are:

$$1 \qquad 17 \qquad 31 \qquad 47$$
$$\text{A} \qquad \text{B} \quad * \quad \text{B}' \qquad \text{A}'$$

An example of foresight, in the articulation of this symmetrical structure, is the way Brahms highlights the axis in the middle of the piece (marked '*' above). The tonal characteristic of the opening material, as shown in Figure 7, is the exclusive and repetitive use of the notes of the scale of 2 sharps. Only on the final semiquaver of the first 4-bar group does Brahms use a chromatic note, Asharp, setting up a tension between D major and B minor which reflects the tonal structure of the piece. The diatonic opening is opposed, almost absolutely, to the chromatic axis, where the cadence bars from 27 to 30 contain all the substitute tones of D except Dsharp — that is, where 11 notes of the chromatic scale are used. The ending returns to diatonic restrictions. Its cadences (61–2 and 65–6) include Asharp, but the descending melodic minor scale of the closing melodic progression recalls the diatonic background of the opening:

Figure 14

This symmetrical structuring, evolved through an opposition implicit in the opening material, is also reflected in the two outer sections. The first pair of 8-bar phrases moves from diatonic to chromatic harmony (cf. 4–8 and 12–16), whereas the chromatic leading notes added to the opening material in its recapitulation (from 47) gradually disappear into the diatonic harmony (with Asharp) at the end.

A second example concerns the octave displacements in the opening material. In the symmetrical relationships shown in Figure 6, the repetitions in the thirds cycle, across 1–2 and 3–4, involve upward displacements, while the cycle itself implies a downward movement over the octave — the cycle produces dissonance and obscures the harmony at its third and fourth steps, that is, at a seventh and ninth from the first note.

These registral characteristics are exploited in several ways. First, the octave structures the melody as a background range. The melody of the first section descends over an octave (cf. 1 and 16). This is reflected less explicitly in the middle section, where the opening (17) and ending (41–3) are an octave apart, but it is emphasized by the descent of the melody at 41 to the octave below middle C (for the first time in the piece). And the melodic progression of the final phrase makes the octave background explicit, as shown in Figure 14.

Second, a symmetrical scheme of octave displacements in the foreground articulates the end of the middle section. The new register of Fsharp in 43 is generated by closely juxtaposed displacements, and Fsharp is a significant note in its position at the head of each phrase (see 1, 9, 17, 31, 47, 55, and, for smaller divisions, 5, 21, 43, 51 and 62):

Figure 15

Finally, the same feature is also active in the overall symmetrical organization, for the opening of the middle section is also registrally structured. The two high E's (24 and 39) are prominent, the first because it is unprepared (and generated by octave displacement), the second because it is never resolved, and they are roughly the same distance on each side of the axis at 30–1:

Figure 16

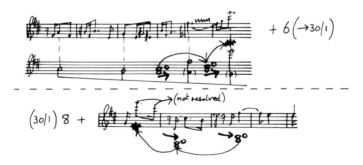

In section XII, Schoenberg examines irregular construction in post-Wagner composers, with examples from Bruckner, Mahler, Strauss, Reger, and his own *Pierrot Lunaire*. The defensive section XIII adds that, even if some of the examples from Brahms and earlier may have been inspired by dramatic and other external influences after all, those from after Wagner are pure musical prose. Irregularity may even have become a norm:

> ...deviations from simple construction...have become incorporated into the syntax and grammar of perhaps all subsequent musical structure. Accordingly, they have ceased to be recorded as merits of a composition. (p. 428)

Section XIV attempts to explain what happened to the progression in the twentieth century, with the conclusion that it seems to have disappeared, though 'the aesthetic background for a just and general judgment has become very questionable at present' (p. 429).

Section XV begins with longer examples showing Brahms's progressive construction. They appealed to Schoenberg because of the freedom in elaborating a motive, at the same time as the strict derivation of this elaboration from the opening ideas. The two analyses are meant to be mutually assertive, for although they identify thematic material which is 'present in every theme' (p. 431), the material is different in each case. Unlike the earlier examples, both are extreme cases from Brahms. This is especially true of the song, *O Tod...*, *Op. 121 No. 3*. Its use of thirds has, as Schoenberg notes (p. 431), a resemblance to the example from the *Fourth Symphony*. But the symphony is an elaborate composition where the thirds are part of a complex of motivic material. *Op. 119i* is less elaborate, but there are still several motivic ideas (see, e.g., the fourths in Figure 12) and motivating relationships (e.g., the octave displacements and diatonic/chromatic opposition discussed above). *O Tod,* however, is a much purer study in thirds: in choosing a more experimental case from Brahms Schoenberg is at his most convincing (see Examples 47–8).

The closing pages of the essay move into more abstract discussion, punctuated by further examples of Brahms's technique. The final technical discussion considers complexities of rhythm, and the good fortune that Brahms did not abandon Mozart's discoveries in the way that Beethoven did (p. 438). The sense of contradiction noted in early stages of the essay is now resolved as Schoenberg drops any defensive attitude in assessing musical structure:

> The idea cannot be rejected that the mental pleasure caused by structural beauty can be tantamount to the pleasure deriving from emotional qualities. (p. 438)

After this, the judgments of Brahms (collected below) are no longer tentative:

...Brahms's merit would be immense, even if he had preserved this way of thinking
only in the manner of a technical device. But — and this characterizes his high rank — he
has surpassed it. (ibid.)

It is important to realize that at a time when all believed in 'expression', Brahms, without renouncing beauty and emotion, proved to be a progressive in a field which had not
been cultivated for half a century. (p. 439)

His influence has already produced a further development of the musical language
toward an unrestricted, though well-balanced presentation of musical ideas. (p. 440)

Finally, Schoenberg sees in Brahms not only a progress which was
already achieved, but a progress which was still to be exploited. Although
'some progress has already been made in this direction' (p. 441), '...the
merits of his achievements will shine brighter when more and more are
incorporated into the dramatic technique' (p. 440).

The essay was clearly not designed as a traditional academic study. It is as
interesting in telling some of Schoenberg's beliefs about his musical roots as
in its examination of Brahms. Nevertheless, the examination is thorough in
the sense that Schoenberg judges on the basis of uncompromising distinctions — between idea and structure, regularity and irregularity, dramatic and
pure music — which are sometimes hard to identify as applied principles, but
which are all stated at least once in an abstract, unambiguous formula.
Where it is less than thorough, it is usually a question of an inappropriate or
unexplained example. There is a contrast, for instance, between the analysis
of *O Tod* and earlier examples (e.g., Example 24), where the music seems
less complex than Schoenberg's explanation would imply. One of the
Mozart examples (Example 51) has stimulated criticism of this kind.
Westergaard is led by Schoenberg to question whether conventional
rhythmic analysis can account for such complicated relationships.[24] But
Cone replies that they are not, in fact, as complicated as Schoenberg shows
in his analysis: Cone's elegant solution[25] is supported by a further contribution in the same debate.[26]
   But this case demonstrates what is perhaps the most attractive and un-
traditional aspect of the essay. Cone was prompted by Schoenberg's com-
ment, that Example 51 is not an enigma to the performer (p. 436). This
casual suggestion of a proper perspective for the example is typical of the
understatement in most of Schoenberg's argument. His analytical approach
is often unhelpful, but his subdued argument makes a convincing and, for
the time, radical tribute to Brahms.

Epilogue

The different analytical approaches in this study reflect both the varying concerns of each chapter and the different material for analysis. For example, the *Handel Variations* provide an opportunity for comparing isolated, but closely related passages of music, which are not found in sonata forms like *Op. 60i* and *Op. 98i*. Similarly, the concern with formal procedure in Chapter 4, though it should be relevant to the mixture of sonata and variation form in *Op. 60i,* would reveal little there of the effect of the music: the different procedures do not seem to be in conflict as they are in *Op. 98i*. It is hoped that each type of analysis, and the limited variety within each type, exploits an opportunity in the music, or focuses on an important aspect of the structure, or, in the case of Chapter 5, is merely illustrative without distorting the nature of the piece.

To the extent that this is achieved, a point is made about the music. With *Op. 60i,* the analysis reflects most directly Schoenberg's claim for Brahms's historical position. The work may be reactionary in many ways — the medium, for instance, was out of fashion by the time of Brahms's middle period, even if the quartet was first conceived at a time (the 1850's) when Schumann had just added several chamber works to the repertoire in a 'progressive' spirit. However, in its harmonic and tonal richness and ambiguity, *Op. 60i* lives up to Schoenberg's notion of a highly developed language, ahead of contemporaneous practice.

The analysis in Chapter 4 makes the closest contact with Brahms's compositional preoccupations. It can be assumed that he was aware of the recurring elements in *Op. 98i* and their effect on sonata procedure: it is not unlikely in view of the Passacaglia which closes the symphony, and the precedent of *Op. 60i,* both of which indicate a deliberate formal mixture. Although this confirms the 'progressive' view that Brahms was concerned with rethinking classical form, it also feeds traditional criticisms. The analysis deals with background relationships of contrapuntal formula, harmonic pattern, and periodicity. This emphasis, and the absence of attention to motivic development, rhythmic shaping, and those features in general which make for what might be called a lyrical style, perhaps reflect the character of the music. Its constructional power, like Brahms's general avoidance of 'mere' melodic variety, is achieved at some expense.

The analysis in Chapter 2 is not designed to say anything about the piece as a whole, except in the sense that, if Brahms meant to express in his letters a desire to manipulate the Theme at many levels of the structure, then the openings of the Variations seem to reveal this concern in the *Handel Variations*. But the analytical method makes a point about the music in comparison with conventional analysis. Assuming that the examination of isolated passages in detail is worthwhile, it proves to be an arduous task using a conventional approach. The oppositional models may highlight the problem of defining a metaphorical relationship to the music, but this is equally a problem in conventional analysis, where in addition the bulk of unsystematic verbal description is an obstacle to the expression of a useful metaphor. The oppositional system was devised, therefore, for the reason that certain music seems to defeat the complex metaphor of conventional analysis: and where oppositional analysis[1] seems more revealing, a distinction is made between this and music amenable to a conventional approach. This is also implied by the illustrations from *Op. 119i*. They show that such unconventional criteria as repetition, symmetry and registral relationship can be crucial in forming an appropriate analytical description. In other words, Brahms sometimes experiments with radical, or as Schoenberg says, progressive manipulations of musical relationships.

Notes

CHAPTER 1

1. K. Geiringer: *Johannes Brahms,* Vienna 1934, p. 189 (trans. here).

2. J. Harrison: *Brahms and his Four Symphonies,* London 1939, pp. 292–93.

3. See below, p. 83.

4. C. Rostand: *Brahms,* Paris 1955, pp. 291–92.

CHAPTER 2

1. See Appendix I.

2. See, e.g., A. Forte: "Schenker's Conception of Musical Structure," Journal of Music Theory 1959.

3. New York 1979 (trans. Ernst Oster), pp. 144–45.

4. O. Jonas: *Einführung in die Lehre Heinrich Schenkers,* Vienna 1972, p. 119.

5. In *Das Meisterwerk in der Musik,* Vol. 2, Munich 1926, pp. 171–92.

6. R.U. Nelson: *The Technique of Variation,* London 1948, p. 124.

7. L.B. Meyer: *Music, the Arts and Ideas,* London 1967, pp. 305-6. The significance of Schenker was that he did relate different levels of the structural hierarchy: the whole point of the background is to show how these levels co-function. However, he set rhythm aside as a special case. See Jonas, op. cit., pp. 9–13.

8. *Langage, Musique, Poésie,* Paris 1972.

9. Ibid., p. 111.

10. For example, the simple contrasts of strict antiphony.

11. Ibid., pp. 109–11.

12. Taking the opening of each variation rather than any two bars in the middle at least provides one valid point of division. It is also worth noting that the first two bars are relatively intact throughout the work; even the Fugue has characteristic 2-bar groupings.

13. See Appendix I.

14. This model has been shifted back a semiquaver in relation to the pulse, beginning with the new semiquaver anacrusis.

15. Brahms: *Briefwechsel* (ed., Deutsche Brahms-Gesellschaft), Berlin 1908–1922.

16. Ibid.

CHAPTER 3

1. C. Rosen: *The Classical Style,* London 1972, p. 41.

2. See, e.g., *Structural Functions of Harmony,* London 1969 (second ed.), p. 36, Example 52 (chords of H). The varying realization of functionally equivalent chords relies on the notion of 'substitute tones', which in turn results from considerations of tonality (see ibid., p. 35). But if Schoenberg traces all relationships to a tonal centre, he nevertheless distinguishes between harmony and tonality.

3. Ibid., p. 11: Schoenberg's brackets.

4. A.T. Katz: *Challenge to Musical Tradition...,* London 1947, p. xxiii.

5. *Harmony,* Chicago 1973 (paperback ed., trans.), p. 255.

6. Schenker's notion of 'incomplete transfer' of structural models in the foreground makes some concession to this problem. For three Brahms examples, see *Free Composition,* op. cit., Figures 110d, 1, 2 and 3.

7. It would therefore seem inappropriate to describe the movement in terms of a pre-determined scheme; see I. Keys: *Brahms Chamber Music,* London 1974: '...but there is never any real prospect of any other than a minor-key ending...' (p. 21).

8. A. Walker: *A Study in Musical Analysis,* London 1962, p. 152.

9. See Chapter 5.

10. These terms are taken from Schoenberg: see *Fundamentals of Musical Composition,* London 1973 (second paperback ed.).

11. The liquidation at the same time introduces arpeggio figures (21, 23) which become important developmental motives in the recapitulation.

12. R.M. Longyear: *Liszt's B minor Sonata, Music Review* 1973, p. 202.

13. The opening of Beethoven's *String Quartet in F major, Op. 59 No. 1,* second movement, is not dissimilar in its ambiguities in the introduction, and swift departure from the tonic first subject. Beethoven goes on, however, to return to the tonic several times before finally leaving it for the second region of the dominant.

14. The genesis of this is discussed in Appendix II.

15. Bare octaves also appear at the end of the exposition (118–21). This formal position reinforces the significance of the other octave markers, in the sense that the basic divisions of the form are articulated by prominent octaves. But the octaves here do not share in the gestural unity of the octave markers.

16. The ability of such small features to play a prominent role is always acknowledged in motivic analysis, but it can be equally evident in formal backgrounds, and the features need not be 'motivic'. Sessions suggests the same idea: 'I could cite many examples where the most essential musical idea...consist(s) not in motifs at all, but in chords, sonorities...or even in single notes of a particularly striking context.' *The Musical Experience,* Princeton 1950, pp. 46–47.

CHAPTER 4

1. Derived from Schoenberg: see p. 93.

2. Cf. Schenker: *Free Composition,* op. cit., Figure 81, 2. Schenker notes the rhythmic progression, but not the octave displacement or the texture.

3. See also the analysis of the opening of *Op. 60i,* Chapter 3.

4. This dominant is resolved on the major I^7 (103).

5. It becomes one of the deviant cadences which join variations in the Finale (see Finale, 216–7).

6. E. Evans: *Handbook to the Chamber and Orchestral Works of Johannes Brahms,* Vol. II, London 1912, p. 152.

CHAPTER 5

1. New York 1950.

2. E.H.W. Meyerstein: *A Master's Testament, Music Review* Vol. 12 (1951), p. 171.

3. A. Goehr: TEMPO No. 114 (1975), p. 25.

4. London 1975. Page numbers refer to this version.

5. W. Dean: *Schoenberg's Ideas, Music & Letters* Vol. XXXI (1950), p. 301.

6. *Musical Quarterly* Vol. XXXVII No. 4 (1951), p. 469.

7. H. Gal: *Johannes Brahms...*, London 1963 (trans.).

8. C.M. Schmidt: *Motivische-thematische Vermittlung...*, Munich 1971.

9. Gal, op. cit., p. 234.

10. Ibid., p. 235.

11. His later concern with 'inspiration' (pp. 406–7) refers to the structural potential of musical ideas rather than their inspired 'beauty' (see below, p. 93).

12. *Structural Functions* (op. cit.) contains Schoenberg's harmonic analysis of the first 86 bars: Example 164, pp. 175–7.

13. Vienna 1911.

14. *The Theoretical Writings of Arnold Schoenberg, Proceedings of the Royal Musical Association* Vol. 100 (1973–74), pp. 95–6.

15. Ibid., p. 96.

16. The idea of 'background' in this sense is examined in Walker, op. cit. A discussion of the different meanings 'background' has had can be found in R.A. Beeson: *Background and Model, Music Review* Vol. 32 (1971).

17. Op. cit., p. 16. See also *Fundamentals*, p. 25, note 1.

18. The 1975 edition misprints 'and *after* simply': cf. 1950 ed., op. cit., p. 68.

19. The following paragraph deals with popularity. It is not about Brahms, though the point it makes is appropriate to his role in the nineteenth century, when such works as the *Hungarian Dances* brought immediate popularity and fame, whereas the most personal compositions, for example *Op. 60,* were never outstandingly successful. The passage is remarkable, however, for Schoenberg's insight into a fundamental quality of music: 'Real popularity, lasting popularity, is only attained in those rare cases where power of expression is granted to men who dwell intensely in the sphere of basic human sentiments' (p. 415). This seems in the essay a casual qualification of the point that 'prolixity alone cannot guarantee general favour', but it is also a kind of self-analysis for Schoenberg. Middleton comes to much the same conclusion about Schoenberg as Schoenberg might have, in applying this *aperçu* to himself. See: *After Wagner, Music Review* Vol. 34 (1973).

20. Brahms's role in the development of irregularity of this kind had been noted at the beginning of the century. See C.F. Abdy Williams: *The Rhythm of Modern Music,* London 1909, p. 134 and Chapters VIII and IX, passim.

21. The second Cello part is more suggestive of $2+2+2+2+2$. The inadequacy of analysing melodies alone is mentioned, for example, in P. Westergaard, *Some Problems in Rhythmic Theory and Analysis, Perspectives of New Music,* Vol. 1 (1962), pp. 180–91 (see note 15).

22. Schoenberg says 'if' this is a principle, but his analyses of rhythm assume it categorically.

23. This is shown to some extent in Chapters 3 and 4.

24. Op. cit., p. 191 (see note 27, which gives Keller's analysis).

25. Ibid., pp. 206-210.

26. W.J. Mitchell, ibid., pp. 210-11.

EPILOGUE

1. Or any other approach which departs from the traditional hierarchy of analytical concerns. Another example might be the Behaviourist methods of Meyer. A similar argument may be found in Eimert's famous essay on Debussy's *Jeux* (Die Reihe, Vol. 5), which implies that analytical convention can be regarded as a comparative test of musical construction.

Bibliography

As the analyses are, in the main, original formulations, the background of literature on analysis and Brahms which has been consulted has little direct bearing on the text. Therefore, only works mentioned in the text and certain books and articles which have proved especially interesting or influential for this study are cited.

Abbreviations

JMT   = Journal of Music Theory
M&L   = Music and Letters
MQ   = Musical Quarterly
MR   = Music Review
MT   = Musical Times
PNM   = Perspectives of New Music
PRMA = Proceedings of the Royal Musical Association

Abdy Williams, C.F., *The Rhythm of Modern Music,* London 1909.
Beeson, R.A., *Background and Model,* MR 1971.
Bernstein, J.A., *An Autograph of the Brahms Handel Variations,* MR 1973.
Brahms, J., *Briefwechsel,* ed. Deutsche Brahms-Gesellschaft, Berlin 1908–1922.
Dale, K., *Brahms,* London 1970.
Dean, W., *Schoenberg's Ideas,* M&L 1950.
Evans, E., *Handbook to the Chamber and Orchestral Works of Johannes Brahms,* London 1912 (2 Vols.).
Forte, A., *The Structural Origin of Exact Tempi in the Brahms Haydn Variations,* MR 1957.
————., *Schenker's Conception of Musical Structure,* JMT 1959.
Gal, H., *Johannes Brahms – His Work and Personality,* London 1963 (trans.).
Geiringer, K., *Johannes Brahms,* Vienna 1934.
Goehr, A., *Review of Style and Idea,* TEMPO 1975 (No. 114).
————, *The Theoretical Writings of Arnold Schoenberg,* PRMA 1973–4 (Vol. 100).
Harrison, J., *Brahms and his Four Symphonies,* London 1939.
Jonas, O., *Einführung in die Lehre Heinrich Schenkers,* Vienna 1972 (second ed.).
Katz, A.T., *Challenge to Musical Tradition – A New Concept of Tonality,* London 1947.
Keys, I., *Brahms Chamber Music,* London 1974.
Leichtentritt, H., *Musical Form,* Cambridge (Mass.) 1951.

Longyear, R.G., *Liszt's B minor Sonata: Precedents...*, MR 1973.

Mann, M., *Schenker's Contribution to Music Theory*, MR 1949.

Matthews, D., *Brahms's Three Phases*, Newcastle 1972.

Mellers, W., *The Sonata Principle*, London 1957.

Meyer, L.B., *Music, the Arts and Ideas*, London 1967.

Meyerstein, E.H.W., *A Master's Testament*, MR 1951.

Middleton, R., *After Wagner*, MR 1973.

Mitschka, A., *Der Sonatensatz in den Werken von Johannes Brahms*, U. of Mainz, dissertation, 1961.

Nelson, R.U., *The Technique of Variation*, London 1948.

Neunzig, H.A., *Johannes Brahms in Selbstzeugnissen und Bilddokumenten*, Hamburg 1973.

Niemann, W., *Brahms*, New York 1929 (trans.).

Pascall, R., *Formal Principles in the Music of Brahms*, U. of Oxford, dissertation, 1972.

———, *Ruminations on Brahms's Chamber Music*, MT 1975.

Rosen, C., *The Classical Style*, London 1972.

Rostand, C., *Brahms*, Paris 1955.

Rubsamen, W.H., *Schoenberg in Ameria*, MQ 1951.

Ruwet, N., *Langage, Musique, Poésie*, Paris 1972.

Schenker, H., *Der Freie Satz*, Vienna 1956. Now available as *Free Composition*, edited and translated by Ernst Oster, New York 1979.

———, *Harmony*, Chicago 1973 (paperback ed., trans.).

———, *Das Meisterwerk in der Musik*, Munich 1925, 26, 30 (3 Vols.; reprinted in 1 Vol., Hildesheim and New York 1974).

Schmidt, C.M., *Motivische-thematische Vermittlung in der Musik von Johannes Brahms*, Munich 1971.

Schoenberg, A., *Fundamentals of Musical Composition*, ed. G. Strang, London 1973 (second paperback ed.).

———, *Harmonielehre*, Vienna 1911.

———, *Structural Functions of Harmony*, London 1969 (second ed.).

———, *Style and Idea*, New York 1950.

———, *Style and Idea*, London 1975.

Sessions, R., *The Musical Experience*, Princeton 1950.

Tovey, D.F., *Essays in Musical Analysis—Chamber Music*, London 1944.

Truscott, H., *Brahms and Sonata Style*, MR 1964.

Urbantschitsch, V., *Die Entwicklung der Sonatenform bei Brahms*, U. of Vienna, dissertation, 1927.

Walker, A., *A Study in Musical Analysis*, London 1962.

Westergaard, P., *Some Problems in Rhythmic Theory and Analysis*, PNM 1962-3 (Vol. 1).

Bibliographic update, 1980

Chapter 2: The *Handel Variations* analysis made no reference to Heinrich Schenker's analysis, which is out of print and rare (*Der Tonwille*, Vol. 8/9, pp. 3–46 and supplement). A description of the scope of Schenker's work on this piece can be read in L. Laskowski's *Heinrich Schenker: An Annotated Index to his Analyses of Musical Works* (New York: Pendragon Press, 1978), p. 78.

Chapter 3:   Two articles by James Webster have provided further information and discussion about the influence of Schubert on Brahms's early sonata form and the genesis of *Op. 60:*
"Schubert's Sonata Form and Brahms's First Maturity," *Nineteenth Century Music,* Vol. 2, No. 1 and Vol. 3, No. 1 (parts I and II).
"The C sharp minor Version of Brahms's Op. 60," *The Musical Times,* Vol. 121, No. 1644, February 1980.

Chapter 5:   A specific analytical study and a more general discussion (which considers both *Op. 98* and *Op. 119*), the first of which was written in the knowledge of the work presented here, the second of which was accidentally missed from the bibliography above:
B. Newbould: "A New Analysis of Brahms's Intermezzo, Op. 119 No. 1," *The Music Review,* Vol. 38, No. 1.
H. Hollander: "Die Terzformel als musikalisches Bauelement bei Brahms," *Neue Zeitschrift für Musik,* Vol. 113, No. 8 (1972).
A recent major study which includes reference to *Brahms the Progressive:*
M. Musgrave: "Schoenberg and Brahms: A Study of Schoenberg's Response to Brahms's Music as Revealed in his Didactic Writings and Selected Early Compositions," Ph.D. dissertation, University of London, 1980.

Index